Angela James

The First Superstar of Women's Hockey

A Biography by
Tom Bartsiokas & Corey Long

Angela James: The First Superstar of Women's Hockey
Tom Bartsiokas & Corey Long

First Published in 2012 by
Women's Press Literary, an imprint of Three O'Clock Press Inc.
180 Bloor St. West, Suite 801
Toronto, Ontario M5S2V6
www.threeoclockpress.com

Every reasonable effort has been made to identify copyright holders. Three O'Clock Press would be pleased to have any errors or omissions brought to its attention.

Three O'Clock Press gratefully acknowledges financial support for our publishing activities from the Ontario Arts Council, and the Government of Canada through the Canada Book Fund. We acknowledge the support of the Canada Council for the Arts which last year invested $20.1 million in writing and publishing throughout Canada.

Library and Archives Canada Cataloguing in Publication

Bartsiokas, Tom, 1975-
Angela James : the first superstar of women's hockey / Tom Bartsiokas and Corey Long.

(Women who rock series ; 5)
ISBN 978-0-9866388-8-6

1. James, Angela, 1964-. 2. Women hockey players—Canada—Biography. 3. Black Canadian hockey players—Biography. 4. Lesbian athletes—Canada—Biography. I. Long, Corey, 1978- II. Title. III. Series: Women who rock series ; 5

GV848.5.J36B37 2012   796.962092   C2012-903089-9

Cover photograph: Copyright © F. Scott Grant/Image Communications
Printed and bound in Ontario, Canada, by: WebCom

WOMEN WHO ROCK | series

Angela James

The First Superstar of Women's Hockey

A Biography by
Tom Bartsiokas & Corey Long

Women's Press Literary
Toronto

♦♦♦

For Christine, Angelina and Deanna. I love you, always and forever.
T.B.

For Shannon and Clara: my hall-of-fame wife and daughter.
With all my love.
C.L.

♦♦♦

FOREWORD
Adam Graves

I was only four years old when I first stepped onto the ice at 165 Grenoble Drive, otherwise known as Flemingdon Park Arena. Little did I know then, this arena would be renamed after one of the most inspirational players hockey has ever known. In 2009, Flemingdon Park Arena was renamed the Angela James Arena. Yes, my friend, Angela James: the same woman I proudly watched, read about and rooted for during her entire career.

Fast-forward 10 years, I was 14 years old working as a gopher at the Seneca College Hockey School. My daily duties included tying skates, cleaning dressing rooms and organizing lunch for the campers. I remember one particular sunny July afternoon. I was on my way to the cafeteria holding an old blue milk basket filled with lunches, when I saw Angela along the way. We exchanged a simple hello and she asked if I was skating that night. I told her I was, and she replied with a "See you there!" As I entered the cafeteria, I couldn't help but ask myself why she was coming to our evening skate. But it all made sense when she stepped onto the ice.

One of the perks of being a Seneca College Hockey School instructor was the two hours of ice time made available to us at the end of each day. We were a staff comprised of different levels of players: Junior B, Major A, college and even some minor pro players. Angela's first shift was one I will never forget. She could skate, pass, shoot, work the corners, see the ice, and she had a slap shot that rivaled anyone. I was a fan—she could really play.

Over the years, we spent hours and hours together working on our game. The Friday night skate was always my favourite. Angela, Stephen Spott (the head coach and general manager of the Kitchener Rangers of the Ontario Hockey League) and I would have the entire ice to ourselves. We would work on our stick handling, passing and, of course, trying to perfect our shots. The same skills that Angela demonstrated on those summer night skates were trademarks of her remarkable Hall of Fame career.

Her accomplishments rank with the best to ever play the game. She was the leading scorer of the COWHL for eight seasons, six-time MVP, and winner of four IIHF World Championship gold medals—this is just a glimpse into her many accolades. Angela played the game of hockey with the same ferocity, passion and completeness that reminded me of a great player, friend and teammate of mine, Mark Messier.

This biography will introduce you to Angela James, the person, allowing the reader to understand her character and appreciate her ability to inspire others by overcoming obstacles on and off the ice. She played her first season as an eight-year-old girl in the all-boys Flemingdon Park Hockey League, finishing the season as the leading scorer. Hurdles and barriers were a way of life for Angela. She met each bit of adversity with the same grit and determination that she exemplified while playing hockey, allowing her to grow as a player and an individual. Her story reinforces the importance of family, sport and education, as well as the important role an educator can play in a student's life.

Angela blazed a trail that opened doors to young girls and women being afforded the opportunity and privilege to play the great game of hockey. Every time my two daughters step onto the ice to play for the Oakville Hornets Girls Hockey Association (which now has over 1,000 players participating) I think of "number eight." I can say, very proudly, thank you Angela for all you have done to benefit the game of hockey. Your passion, humility and respect for hockey has inspired us all. Congratulations on your induction into the Hockey Hall of Fame. Simply put, your "no. 8" is exactly where it belongs!

Adam Graves is an 18-year NHL veteran; 1,152 games played; 329 goals; 287 assists; two-time Stanley Cup champion.
His number nine jersey was retired by the New York Rangers in 2009.

Adam playing for the Flemingdon Kings.

CHAPTER 1

"This Is The Call"

In the days leading up to the announcement of the 2010 Hockey Hall of Fame inductees, many potential names were bandied about. That year's class would be especially intriguing because, in March 2009, the Hall updated its procedure for electing new members. The ultimate shrine for the game's immortals would now consider men and women independently. Up to four men and two women could now be inducted each year.

As anticipation grew, the name that seemed to be on everybody's lips was Angela James. The mixed-race daughter of an absentee black American father and a devoted mother, Angela grew up in government-funded housing, not exactly fitting the pedigree of a typical Canadian hockey player. Yet from the early 1980s through the mid-1990s, she was the most dominant female player on the planet. As a star for various teams in the Central Ontario Women's Hockey League (COWHL) and the Canadian women's national ice hockey team, Angela scored, hit and battled her way to the top of the game, striking fear in opponents and earning the admiration of teammates and coaches.

Angela's unlikely rise to hockey stardom began when she was a child playing shinny against grown men in the east Toronto neighbourhood of Flemingdon Park. She had played on borrowed skates, staying out until it was too dark to see—just as Wayne Gretzky had done on the backyard rink his father built. Yet Angela did not have Gretzky's sheltered childhood and stable family life. She played to avoid the pitfalls that can catch children in hazardous environments like Flemingdon Park.

In "the Park," drugs were readily available, kids were tough and not afraid to fight, and single parents like Angela's mother struggled to make ends meet. As a young girl, Angela was also an outsider in her own game. When she was eight years old, her domination of the local boy's house league made her unwelcome. Her presence made parents feel uncomfortable. They resented that their boys were easily being outplayed by this scrawny girl with dark skin.

At age 10, with no female players in her age group able to match her skill, Angela played in a girl's league for 13-year-olds. Four years later, Angela joined the COWHL and played with women almost twice her age. She was named COWHL MVP six times and was its top scorer eight times. She started college at just 16 and set Ontario Colleges Athletic Association (OCAA) scoring records as a defence-man, eventually having her no. 8 retired by the OCAA and her alma mater, Seneca College.

Although AJ, as her friends call her, was a defenceman in col-lege, for most of her playing career, she was a centreman. She was a big, tough power forward, with the instincts of a gifted playmaker. Angela scored at will, saw the ice exceptionally well and was an in-timidating physical presence. Angela was a member of the inaugural Canadian women's national hockey team in 1990, leading the team to four consecutive world championships in 1990, 1992, 1994, and 1997. In 20 games for Team Canada, Angela scored 22 goals, includ-ing a two-goal performance in the 1994 world championship final against the United States.

Angela's career did not come without some disappointments, however. In 1998, at age 33, she was left off the inaugural Canadi-an Women's Olympic Hockey team. Canada, the favourite to win gold, came home with only silver. Angela's absence was considered a major factor in the loss and the decision not to have her on the team remains controversial today. Those familiar with the women's game, including CBC commentator and former hockey player Robin Brown, contend that without Angela, women's hockey would never have been included in the Olympics.[1] On that basis alone, she should have earned a spot on the roster. Being cut from the Olympic team was a bitter moment in an otherwise exceptional career that saw An-gela set herself apart from contemporaries throughout the 1980s and 1990s.

With the support of her family, her undying determination, her natural athletic gifts and passion for hockey, Angela overcame the obstacles that were presented during her childhood, both on and off the ice. She became the first female hockey superstar in Canada, even earning the nickname, "the Wayne Gretzky of women's hockey."

After Angela's retirement in 2001, the accolades continued to roll in: the Black Ice Hockey and Sports Hall of Fame, the Canada's Sports Hall of Fame and even the Canadian Ball Hockey Association Hall of Fame. Along with Geraldine Heaney and Cammi Granato, she was one of the first female inductees into the International Ice Hockey Federation Hall of Fame. As well, in 2009, Flemingdon Park honoured Angela by renaming its arena the Angela James Arena. From that day forward, every little girl in Flemingdon Park with a dream of playing hockey would have a hero to look up to each time she walked through the doors of her neighbourhood arena. Would the Hockey Hall of Fame be next?

Prior to the announcement on June 22, 2010, the last thing on Angela James' mind was the Hockey Hall of Fame. Along with her partner, Angela McDonald (who AJ lovingly refers to as "Ange"), she was busy raising their three children, Christian, Michael and Toni. She was also coaching and refereeing hockey (as she had done since her teens), coordinating intramural sports at Seneca College, public speaking and volunteering. As well, Angela had been playing in a recreational men's league with former junior players, some of them half her age—a reversal from her beginnings as a small girl playing with the men in Flemingdon Park. "I wasn't even thinking about it," remembers Angela. "It wasn't until the day before when all the media started calling and it was starting to get really crazy. They were calling in anticipation, asking me, 'Will this happen?' And I was like, 'Will you talk to me if it doesn't?'"

Angela had reason to be sceptical. The procedure for induction into the Hockey Hall of Fame is one of the most rigorous in sports. An 18-person committee, handpicked by the Hall, debates all the candidates submitted for consideration. Anyone can put forward a candidate, but an inductee requires 14 of the 18 members' votes to get in. So, even with the new rules allowing women to be considered separate from men, if no female candidate received 14 votes, the Hall would remain an all-boys club for at least another year.

The 2010 edition of the selection committee, at first glance, was not one that would seem overly sympathetic to, or knowledgeable about, women's hockey. The all-male group was heavy with NHL alumni, including Pat Quinn, Scotty Bowman, Lanny McDonald, Peter Stastny and Harry Sinden. Among the hockey writers on the committee was Eric Duhatschek of The Globe & Mail. Three years earlier, Duhatschek had written that perennial Team Canada captain and Olympic gold medalist Cassie Campbell-Pascall, not Angela James, was better suited for induction into Canada's Sports Hall of Fame. "Sadly I didn't see much of James as a player," he wrote. "As a pioneer, I'm sure she opened some doors for the [Hayley] Wickenheisers, the [Lindsay] Hoffords and the [Jennifer] Botterills [...] but in all that time that women's hockey slowly built a profile and a presence for itself across Canada and the United States, no one was more synonymous with the sport than Cassie Campbell-Pascall."[2] As Duhatschek predicted Cassie was inducted into the Canada's Sports Hall of Fame a year ahead of Angela. Would history repeat itself? Or would they consider someone else for the honour?

Indeed, as the number of women's hockey leagues grew beginning in the late 1970s, many players had, like Angela and Cassie, distinguished themselves as worthy of consideration. To name just a few: the outstanding American goal scorer Cammi Granato; Shirley Cameron, who was instrumental in developing women's hockey in western Canada; Geraldine Heaney, the best defenceman of her generation. Or would recent stars have to wait their turns until the game's pioneers were recognized, such as Lord Stanley's daughter Isobel, who fostered women's hockey in the nineteenth century?

Regardless of who would be the first, the fact that women hockey players were now seen as separate, but equal to their male colleagues in the eyes of the Hall was a victory for women's hockey in Canada as well as globally. The countless players, officials and administrators who championed women's hockey, who fought for equal ice time, funding and national support, would now see their own heroes recognized alongside the game's greatest male players.

The day the committee made its decision, Angela was at home with Ange. As it turns out, June 22 is their anniversary. While the phone was ringing off the hook with interview requests, both became more and more excited about a potential trip to the Hall.

Angela thought about the many times she'd taken groups of young hockey players to the Hockey Hall of Fame—that beautiful 1885 heritage building at the corner of Yonge and Front Streets in Toronto's downtown core. Each visit, she was in awe of the tributes bestowed on the heroes of her youth: Guy Lafleur, Lanny McDonald, Darryl Sittler and Mark Messier. But at the same time, Angela was also saddened that the displays commemorating women's hockey were minimal and that there were no females in the Hockey Hall of Fame to inspire young women. She could only imagine how that would change if the Hall ever inducted a woman.

That change was announced to the world at 3:20 p.m., on the day of Ange and Angela's anniversary. Angela had found out about an hour earlier. Sprawled out on the couch in the middle of a phone interview with CBC Television, she excused herself to answer her cell phone. The CBC was happy to wait. "This is Bill Hay, Chair of the Hockey Hall of Fame…" said the voice on the other phone.

"Then he started talking," recalls Angela. "And I didn't really get it at first. I said, 'Oh my God.' Ange was right there and I whispered to her, 'This is the call.' Then I had to return to the CBC interview on the other line as if I didn't know anything."

After hugging Ange, Angela immediately called her mother with instructions to let her siblings know, but not to tell anyone else for at least another hour—not an easy task for Angela's biggest lifelong fan. Angela then told some close friends and tried to make sense of the phone call she had received. The Hockey Hall of Fame. First woman ever inducted. Second black player. A permanent home alongside hockey's immortals. It wasn't her victories with the Canadian national women's team or her dominance in the Central Ontario Women's Hockey League that occupied her mind. Instead, she thought about playing as a child, learning the game in Flemingdon Park and the unorthodox cast of characters that helped her along the way. If it takes a village to raise a child, it takes a village with a sheet of ice to raise a hockey player.

CHAPTER 2

Survival Mode

Angela Gladys Diane James was born on December 22, 1964 at Toronto General Hospital.

Earlier that year, the Beatles conquered America and Sidney Poitier became the first black man to win the Oscar for Best Actor in a Leading Role. Arthur Ashe broke the colour barrier to become a member of the United States Davis Cup tennis team, and South Africa was banned from the Olympic Games because of its apartheid policies. The Toronto Maple Leafs defeated the Detroit Red Wings to win their third straight Stanley Cup, and Gordie Howe scored his 545th goal, passing Maurice "Rocket" Richard on the way to 801 career goals—second all-time behind Wayne Gretzky.

Angela entered the world under trying circumstances. Her mother, Donna Baratto, was already a single parent living in a government subsidized apartment in Scarborough, Ontario, with her two daughters, five-year-old Cindy, and 18-month-old Kym. Donna also had two sons named Bobby and Larry.

It was an unexpected and difficult pregnancy for Donna. Due to complications, she was bedridden for months before Angela's birth and then was forced to stay in the hospital a month after Angela was born. This difficult beginning forged an immediate bond between the two. From the moment Angela arrived, she was the apple of her mother's eye.

When Angela was 18 months old, the family moved into a larger subsidized townhouse in Toronto, at the intersection of Don Mills Road and Eglinton Avenue—the neighbourhood known as Flemingdon Park. To raise the girls on her own, Donna needed government assistance. Neither Angela's father nor the fathers of her sisters provided financial support, and Donna received no help from her own family. Mother and daughters shared a unit in a townhouse at 6 Vendome Place.

Donna remembers Angela as being very pleasant and shy as a child, but quick to anger and always ready to defend her sisters and friends if anyone were to cross them. She states with pride that Angela was walking by seven months and that she knew very early her daughter was destined for a life in sports. "When she received her first holy communion, her godfather gave Angela her first bat and glove," says Donna. "From then on, it was only sports."

Angela was a tomboy from the beginning. She hated dresses and pigtails—anything "girly." Having her hair brushed was torture, and her mother used to braid it so much it started to thin out. Finally, Donna's good friend "Aunt" Mickey Harris urged her to cut Angela's hair once and for all. "Chop it off!" she insisted. That's exactly what happened, and Angela has worn it short ever since.

As both the baby and the gifted athlete in the family, Angela admits to being spoiled and quite sheltered by her mother, though that didn't stop her from having a rough-and-tumble childhood that would be mirrored in her hockey career. When she was two years old, Angela was already able to ride a bicycle, though she had yet to master stopping. She "borrowed" her brother's bike—which was certainly too big for her—and drove it into the side of the family's townhouse, knocking out her front tooth. When her new tooth finally arrived years later, she knocked it out, too, this time while chasing her sister down a hallway: all that waiting for nothing. A false tooth was needed, which she would always take out before hockey games. "It was a good thing I got the school dental plan," says Donna. "Thank God. It would have been $1,000 for one tooth!"

Angela's special relationship with Donna also had to do with the fact that she was her mother's fifth and last child—her baby. All five children were born to different fathers. Larry was put up for adoption, while Bobby lived with his father, Donna's ex-husband. None of the girls' dads had a consistent role in their upbringing. The burden on Angela's mother to care for them was extremely heavy and sometimes too much for her to bear.

❖❖❖

Donna, whose maiden name is McKay, was born in 1934. She is the daughter of a Scottish mortgage broker and a nurse. She grew up in Toronto at Dufferin Street and St. Clair Avenue—an area known as "Corso Italia" due to its many Italian inhabitants. She was the third of four children, with two older sisters and a brother. When Donna was a young girl, the family moved to the bedroom community of Port Credit, just west of Toronto.

A lifelong hockey fan, Donna remembers going to many Toronto junior games—the Marlboros and St. Michael's Majors—when she was in school. Her love of sports was passed down to her children. "My dad got us season's tickets," says Donna. "And I'd go and watch the boys play in the outdoor arenas. I used to sneak out of school to see the games."

Donna was not one to play by the rules, especially those in place for girls her age. Sneaking out of school to watch the boys play hockey was just the beginning. She was disowned by her parents at 16 because they could not control her and disapproved of her choice of an Italian boyfriend, who eventually became her husband. Donna was fiercely independent, stubborn and unwilling to conform to the norms for women in post–World War II Canada. Her mother would later say her daughter was born "ahead of her time." Donna married young, and she and her husband, a traditional man, had Bobby. Despite Donna's troubles with her side of the family, they would always welcome Bobby with open arms.

Donna's marriage was not meant to be. Her husband had as much luck conforming her to traditional female roles as her parents did. Donna's mother and father attempted to reconcile their differences with their daughter, but after she got pregnant with her second son, Larry, through a relationship outside her marriage, they disengaged again.

Larry, who is half black like Angela, was put up for adoption but established a relationship with Donna and her children 18 years later. By chance, Larry met his half-brother Bobby at school. They even played hockey together. Larry had kept his mother's last name, which is how he and Bobby came to know each other, making the connection through their common surname. "Larry was adopted. We always knew he was out there. It wasn't a surprise when he found us," remembers Angela's sister Kym. "He was our brother, and we accepted him."

Over the years, Donna would re-establish ties with her parents, eventually remaining in constant contact with her mother and making peace with her father before his death. Donna's daughters would even be welcomed occasionally at her parents' cottage—except Angela, who never seemed to get an invitation. As a child, Angela thought nothing of it, probably because she was so busy playing sports. Going to a cottage would interfere with softball, swimming or ball hockey. Later, Angela realized what was really going on. "They would take Kym to their cottage. And I was stupid. I didn't understand until I was an adult what was taking place," says Angela. "Kym and I would talk, and I'd ask her, 'How can our grandparents take you to their cottage and treat you like gold, but never take me?' It was because I was black."

Donna's parents' reluctance to accept Angela added to the distance between them and contributed to the isolation Donna was experiencing in all areas of her life. As a divorcé raising three girls alone, Donna's prospects for work and relationships were limited. While living in government housing, she would work low-paying jobs to make ends meet, including the overnight shift at a downtown Toronto hotel.

More than once, the pressure was too much for Donna; she would suffer from depression and nervous breakdowns. According to her daughters, Donna conveyed in later years that it is quite possible that an undiagnosed mental illness led to many of her troubles as a teenager and young adult. With no real help from the fathers of any of her children, Angela's included, Donna's illnesses often forced her to leave her girls with babysitters and friends.

◆◆◆

Angela's father, Leo James, came to Canada from rural Mississippi at age 16 in search of a better life. Leo was raised by his mother and father, who picked cotton for a living, and he claims to have many brothers and sisters. He was an amateur boxer growing up, but admits he's never put on a pair of skates.

"Back in those days, there was so much prejudice down there," says Leo. "You couldn't drink from the same fountain, you couldn't sit and eat at restaurants. Everything was wrong. When I got to Toronto I saw everyone was mixed together. So, I said, 'Well, this has got to be the right place.'"

When he decided to leave Mississippi, he didn't tell his parents. His departure was hastened by an incident where he spoke to a white female shopkeeper while buying a soda. This was forbidden, and the white men in the town came after him with the intention of hanging him. He escaped to South Carolina, then made his way to Canada via Niagara Falls, and ended up in Toronto. Leo did not enter Canada legally, and he was deported three times before obtaining a work permit and finding work as a railway porter.

Leo would talk to Angela and her sisters about how far he had come from the boy who left segregation and racism in the south, coming to Canada, "with no shoes on my feet." He learned to survive and take advantage of any situation with his guile and engaging personality. He was involved with a Toronto nightclub called The 3 J's and, as it turned out, many of the women who visited there. Leo was a good-looking, charming man, who loved to love women but was never in relationships for the long haul. By Leo's estimation, Angela has approximately nine half-siblings through him, five of whom she is in touch with. Angela believes this number to be closer to 15, and that one of her half-brothers is Theo Peckham, a defenceman with the Edmonton Oilers.[1]

Angela describes her father as a "ladies man" and a "tough guy," who came in and out of her life at will, but would be there in a heart-beat if Angela needed him. In one instance, Angela recalls being "smacked" by a man in her neighbourhood when she was a little girl, simply because she was black. Her mother then told Leo who showed up with a group of friends to straighten this guy out. "If you even see Angela," Leo told the man, "you had better walk on the other side of the street." That man never bothered Angela again.

The consensus among Donna's three daughters is that Leo was the love of her life. She would date other men, but none of them were good enough; none of them was Angela's father. When Angela was very young, her mother and father attempted a relationship, but it was not to be. Leo simply refused to settle down, and this left a hole in Donna's life that took many years for her to get over. She admits wasting what she called the best part of her life on him. "He was my life," says Donna. "Now, I think back about what an old fool I was."

Although Leo was absent for the better part of Angela's upbring-ing, he was the most visible of both of her sisters' fathers. Cindy and Kym recall him appearing from time to time, always treating them "as equals." Cindy remembers Leo as the closest thing to a father she ever had; he taught her how to dance, and she used to call him "Daddy Leo." Angela contends that Leo never denied that she was his daughter, although he did not contribute financially during her childhood. And while her mom and sisters became smitten by his charms, Angela seemed to know better and was always aware of Leo's limits as a father and caregiver. "I knew enough as a kid not to let him get close," says Angela. "He doesn't know what it's like to be a parent."

Leo contends that, although he and Donna "wanted different

things," he and Angela were close during her childhood. "We had a good relationship," he says. "It was a distant one because I wasn't living with her mama."

Angela's relationship with her father was a case of "you can't miss what you've never had." All that she knew was a house full of women and girls. Although she met her father and understood who he was, the idea of a man who lived with the family full-time was foreign to her and her sisters, none of whom had ever lived with their fathers. And although it was a household of limited resources, there was no lack of love among Donna and her children. They tended to gravitate to Donna, regardless of where they were. It was a house where music was always playing. Donna introduced her girls to Motown and ingrained a love of music in them early, which Angela would later bring to her own children.

Donna tended to gather people from outside the family. There were always folks in and out of the townhouse—a collection of "extended" family members, for whom Donna would cook and care. Barbecues with Donna's friends and their children were the norm. These people would become more like family to the girls than their own aunts and uncle. When she was well, Donna would also become the go-to babysitter for anyone in need of a night out. Not a big partier herself, she always made her home available, day or night.

The love Donna showed her children and those around her was obvious to everyone. Family was a priority for her, which made her alienation from her own parents even more heartbreaking. Her collection of dependants was an attempt to make up for the loss of her biological family and a way of telling her daughters, "What happened to me will never happen to you." Donna's daughters took this example to heart.

Cindy, the oldest daughter, was born in 1959. At the time Donna was in a relationship with a man who she briefly lived with. Although never really a part of her life, Cindy knew her father, and he would "pop in and out" until she was about 14. She claims not to have known him very well or to have wanted to either. When Cindy was about three, there was a period when she was taken to a foster home because Donna was suffering from depression and could not care for her. She also lived with her grandparents for a time. "My mom was sick when I was growing up," says Cindy. "She had a lot of problems with mental illness."

Whenever Donna experienced episodes of mental illness, the girls were taken away to different homes. Cindy was always the first one to go back; she was the oldest and had a strong relationship with her mother, always respecting that Donna did the best she could for her daughters. Being the oldest by a few years, Cindy was less of a sister and more of a mother to Angela and Kym, and would often play peacemaker between the two. While Donna was working or ill, Cindy did all the babysitting, beginning at age nine. From an early age, she did her best to protect Angela. "All she had to do was yell, 'Cindy!' And I'd come running to beat the crap out of Kym," says Cindy.

By the time Cindy was 16, she was working two part-time jobs, often providing Donna with money to help cover the family's expenses. Three years later, she would move in with her boyfriend, Gary, and the two married when Cindy was 22. They raised three children, later divorcing when Cindy was 36. Although Cindy cared for her mother and sisters deeply, she was anxious to get out on her own and have her independence. She admits to perhaps rushing into marriage to escape the pressures of her family life, yet even then she was a source of support and funds for her mother and sisters.

Being older, Cindy feels she missed out on a lot of Angela and Kym's growing up. Busy working, she never related to them as sisters until all three were adults and mothers themselves. "Kym and Angela had a lot in common," says Cindy. "They did a lot of things together, and Kym took her everywhere, to all of her games."

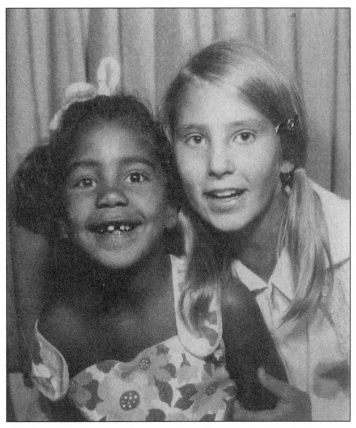

Angela showing off that missing tooth with her sister Cindy.

Kym, born just 18 months before Angela, was her best friend grow-ing up despite their constant scraps. The two were inseparable. Kym experienced many hardships from an early age; she suffered from osteogenesis imperfecta (or brittle bone disease), which limited her ability to keep up with her athletic sister. Despite being the older sib-ling, Kym recalls always looking up to Angela and wanting to be like her. But it was sometimes difficult to watch her younger sister receive a great deal of attention and support while excelling in her many sporting activities. Admittedly, Kym was a little jealous of Angela's relationship with Donna, feeling at times that their mother loved Angela more.

To make matters worse, Kym never knew her father. The circumstances behind her birth are unclear and not something Donna wishes to remember or discuss. Kym speculates her mother became pregnant with her as the result of a sexual assault which Donna suffered while working as a cleaning woman. "I was told my mother could have had an abortion, but she kept me," says Kym. "I have so much love for her."

Kym describes herself as a happy-go-lucky toddler, but that changed at age five when she became the victim of molestation at the hands of a man whose wife babysat the girls and was a trusted friend of the family. Cindy also recalls this man attempting to abuse her on one occasion. Angela, who would have been three at the time of these attacks, does not remember anything similar happening to her. Donna sensed something was wrong with her daughter and, through counselling, the cause of Kym's change in behaviour was revealed. The man responsible was caught and run out of Flemingdon Park by the men who lived there. "He was gone in a week or two," says Cindy. "The men in our neighbourhood went after him. If my mom hadn't been there, they probably would have killed him."

This experience would haunt Kym throughout her adolescence and adulthood. By the time she was eight, Kym was rebellious and uncontrollable. She'd steal from Cindy, and her mother could not handle her. She was placed in the Hincks Treatment Centre, a group home in Mississauga, Ontario. This may have made matters worse; Kym was one of the youngest at the home and was exposed to older children who influenced her negatively. She felt the stigma of being a "group home kid." Later, when Cindy would catch Kym stealing from her, she would claim innocence, saying, "I get blamed for everything because I was in a group home."

Things would get worse before they got better for Kym. She left the family for two years during her teens, living on the street—a period she describes as "two years of hell." She then rejoined the family and re-established relationships with her sisters that remain strong to this day. In dealing with her demons and confronting the events that so drastically changed her life as a child, Kym found strength in her mother's devotion. She is now a mother herself, to a son and daughter, and works as a teacher's assistant. She credits her mother for the accomplishments of all three sisters: "We had love and all turned out to be good kids," says Kym. "No criminals or drug addicts. We've done pretty good."

Flemingdon Family (left to right): Larry, Angela, Cindy, Bobby, Donna and Kym.

Due to the efforts of her mother and sisters to shelter her from the realities the family was facing, Angela remembers her childhood as fun. Yet she also acknowledges that it was not normal, thanks to her unorthodox family situation. When things were going badly, she'd escape through sports. By age seven she was into hockey, baseball and synchronized swimming. She was a natural at all three. It broke her mother's heart that she did not continue with synchronized swimming because she was so good at it.

Angela and her family also found some support through the Saint Bonaventure Catholic Church, which is located minutes from Flemingdon Park. Saint Bonaventure provided opportunities for activities which complemented Angela's constant athletic involvement. The church was also helpful in other ways. When Donna was ill, a nun from the church would stay with the girls at the townhouse. Unaware of what was going on, Angela would ask for her mother and complain about the steady diet of powdered mashed potatoes the nun would serve. Angela called her every name in the book and even chased her with a knife. "The nun made them every night for six weeks, and I remember losing it," says Angela. "She was yelling at me, telling me she was going to tell the priest. I told her to tell him. I was going to tell him that she was torturing me by making me eat mashed potatoes every night."

Angela would "lose it" on more than one occasion during her childhood, with a temper that would become her trademark on the ice. Although sheltered, Angela was also acutely aware of her environment and not an innocent by any means. Sporting activities were complemented with sling shots, thrown marbles, fighting, stealing and, at times, drug and alcohol use.

Angela would attribute her temper to constantly being in what she calls "survival mode" throughout her childhood and adolescence; whether in dust-ups with her sisters or the other kids in the Park, she was always on guard. On the ice and on the street, Angela was often left without parental supervision and had to fend for herself, her sister and her friends—it shaped her personality as an athlete and an adult. As well, Angela was one of the very few black children in Flemingdon Park at the time and people would ridicule her, making her doubt her family lineage, telling her that there was no way a black girl could have a white mother and sisters. "You were constantly fighting for who you are," says Angela. "You were always fighting for your identity."

CHAPTER 3

The Park

The neighbourhood of Flemingdon Park was meant to serve as the blueprint for all future Toronto high-rise communities. The one square mile of farmland was owned by Toronto Mayor R.J. Fleming in the late 1800s. It cost more than $300 million to develop and was modeled after similar "apartment cities" in Europe.[1] By the early 1970s, one concrete building after another popped up in the area east of Don Mills Road and north of the Don Valley Parkway. In the middle of this mushroom crop of apartments were semi-detached homes, townhouses and government housing units that gave families like Angela's a chance at a fresh start. "Everybody knew we lived in Ontario Housing," says Angela. "But we were all in the same boat and that's what made the neighbourhood unique."

"The Park," as Angela and her friends nicknamed it, was a relatively safe place for families to raise their children when Angela was young. From morning to night, Angela and her crew of self-described "misfits" would run wild around the area without any fear of abduction or parental curfews. Many nights, Angela and her friends camped out in the neighbourhood instead of returning back home to sleep in their warm beds. Their favourite evening pastime was breaking into the local outdoor pool for late-night swims. They were never caught, but word did get back to some of the parents, including Donna. Instead of punishing the kids, the grownups decided to join in on the fun. Angela, Kym and their pals even cut a hole in the fence because their moms couldn't scale the metal barrier. This worked out especially well for Angela, who would wake up before anyone else in the morning to collect any loose change that fell into the pool. The Flemingdon Park pool holds a number of special memories for the family, but it is also the place where Angela experienced the first major tragedy of her life.

It was the middle of the day and Angela and her crew decided to head to the pool for an afternoon swim. All the lifeguards and staff knew Angela and her friends by name. The kids were having fun and horsing around when one of the lifeguards blew his whistle and instructed everyone to evacuate the pool. Soon after, a young boy was pulled unconscious from the water after hitting his head while jumping in. Angela saw the tragedy unfold first hand. As she stood there, in shock, the boy eventually haemorrhaged and died before her eyes. The memory of that little boy's death has remained with Angela her entire life.

As a result of this tragic incident, the city closed the pool. Soon after, Angela and her friends found other activities to occupy their time, including petty crime and recreational drug use. Money was scarce at home, and Angela and her sisters had no choice but to steal food and other supplies they needed to survive. Growing up, their favourite places to rip off were the local supermarket, doughnut shop, as well as a nearby cola factory.

Angela, Kym and the rest of their crew hit the supermarket and doughnut shop during the day for milk, bread and sugary treats. When it got dark, they robbed the cola factory. By then all the trucks were loaded with cases of pop—easy pickings for Angela and her friends, who only had to hop a single fence, climb into the trucks and grab as many cans as they could possibly stuff into their clothes.

In all their years of robbing these places, Angela and her friends never got arrested. The closest they came to getting caught was one night at the cola factory when a security guard spotted them and gave chase. Everyone got away except for Kym, who was a little bigger than the rest of the kids and couldn't quite make it over the fence in time. When Angela looked back to see what had happened to her sister, she couldn't believe her eyes: Kym had pushed the poor security guard to the ground and got away. "We were little thieves back then," confesses Angela. "Mom would ask, 'Where are you going?' And we'd always say, 'Oh, we're going to rob the factory.'"

When Angela and Kym would return home from their Park adventures they would often find their house buzzing with people. Cindy always had friends over, and Donna never turned away anyone who showed up at her front door. Over the years, different people often stayed with the family for extended periods, including Angela's brothers. Angela recalls meeting her brother Larry for the first time after school one day. She opened the door and there he was, sitting in the living room watching TV. "Who are you?" asked Angela. "That's your brother Larry," replied Donna.

It was moments like these that reminded Angela that her family was not exactly normal. But even with all the chaos at home, money troubles, and an absentee father, Angela never wished she lived anywhere else or belonged to another family. "We may not have had a lot," says Angela, "but we had lots of love."

Angela with her sister Kym in Flemingdon Park.

Angela relied on the love and support of her mother and sisters on a number of occasions. Often, she had to deal with the racism that came with being the only black child growing up in Flemingdon Park in the 1970s. There were those who questioned whether or not she was adopted because they couldn't believe this little girl with black skin and curly black hair really was part of an all-white family. There was also the name calling and racial slurs that Angela was forced to listen to at the rink, schoolyard and all around the neighbourhood. Names like "nigger" and "blackie" were hurled her way from kids and adults alike. On one occasion, Donna remembers coming home to find Angela scrubbing her arm in the tub. When Donna asked Angela what she was doing, she replied, "I'm trying to get the dirt off. They told me I was dirty." "Who?" asked Donna. "The kids at the school," answered Angela.[2]

As she got older, Angela turned to her fists to deal with anyone who made fun of her skin colour. It didn't matter if it was a boy or a girl, younger or older; anyone who called Angela "nigger" was greeted with a fight. Angela recalls one particular incident when a group of Jamaican girls taunted her for being "different." They had just moved to the neighbourhood and questioned Angela's ethnicity. "They were like, 'You are not black, you are not white, what are you?'" recalls Angela.

The conversation quickly got heated and before Angela knew it, the group took her to the ground and repeatedly kicked her. This was one of the few times Angela remembers losing a dust-up. Needless to say, she wasn't happy. "I got each and every one of them back, one at a time," she says. "That was the only way I could do it." Fighting was part of Angela's life in the Park, just like hockey. But Donna never condoned her daughter's need to get back at those who taunted her. Instead, she always encouraged Angela to walk away with her "head held high."

Although she had to endure these taunts and resort to her fists now and then, Angela had a lot of fun growing up in Flemingdon Park. For her and her friends, the Park was a giant playground to be explored, and that's exactly what they did. They stayed out late doing just about anything they wanted, including experimenting with the drugs and alcohol that were readily available. Before she was 15, Angela admits to trying her share of substances, but never became a chronic user because of her love of sport. For Angela, there was no greater high than playing and competing. While she excelled at pretty much everything she tried, her drug of choice was hockey.

Growing up, there was never a day that Angela wasn't outside playing hockey. It was the first thing she did after school and the only thing she did on the weekends. In the summer, she would play ball hockey with her friends on the street or tennis court. When the season changed to winter, she'd take her game to the ice. Angela also spent a lot of time in her formative years playing softball. The first organized sports team she ever belonged to was a softball team when she was six years old. Her sister's were on it too, and this was the first and only time Donna's girls ever played on an organized team together. Angela really liked softball. She was exceptionality good at all aspects of the game and would eventually play at the college level. But she loved hockey—it's what she lived for.

Angela started playing hockey at six. She cut her teeth playing street hockey before moving to the ice two years later. At first, none of the neighbourhood kids would let her play. They were all older and couldn't understand why a little girl would want to participate against boys in such a rough and tumble sport. So Angela watched and waited, hoping she would be asked to join. When that fateful day finally arrived, Angela was told she would have to play in goal. She didn't mind. She just wanted to play. Without any equipment on, Angela stood her ground and did her best to keep the tennis ball out of the net. This meant taking the occasional shot off the forehead, which Angela laughs off today as a rite of passage for any future hockey star.

Finally, after paying her dues in net, the guys saw that this black girl from the government-owned townhouse was serious. Soon enough, she was mixing it up as a forward with the rest of the little road warriors. Later, as her passion for the game grew, Angela would be the one to organize all the neighbourhood street hockey games thanks to the collection of nets, sticks and balls she had "scrounged" together. "We played from morning until night," recalls Angela. "I always say those commercials with the kids playing road hockey and screaming, 'Car!' That was us."

Everything she knew about the game, Angela learned on her own from watching and playing. Whenever there wasn't a game to be played, she'd take that time to work on her hockey skills like stick handling and shooting. Over and over again, Angela would slap a tennis ball up against the wall, or in the parking garage, perfecting early on what would become one of the most feared and respected slap shots in women's hockey. Every day, like clockwork, her routine was 100 shots on her forehand followed by 100 shots on her backhand. Years later, she'd preach this dedication to the countless children she coached, promising them they'd improve if they took those 200 shots each day. "I just loved hockey. I loved watching it and I loved playing it," says Angela. "I loved being around friends who played it. If you played hockey, I'd just join in."

Even from a distance, Angela's father saw his daughter's passion for hockey from the time she started playing on the streets of Flemington Park. Although hockey wasn't his kind of sport, he encouraged Angela whenever he could.

"From the beginning, that's all she did, day and night: hockey, hockey, hockey," says Leo. "I was proud of her, because she did what she wanted to do."

When summer turned to fall, and fall turned to winter, the street hockey games ended and the games on Flemingdon Park's outdoor rink began. Just like with street hockey, Angela hit the ice and taught herself the basics, including how to skate. There wasn't a coach or father in the crowd shouting out instructions to her, Angela just watched and learned. Whenever she fell to the ice, she'd get back up and try again. There was no quit in her—a trait that would later define her career. After hours of skating, her feet would always be throbbing due to the old pair of skates a neighbour named Johnny

Murray had given her. They were black and yellow and so old that Angela had to curl her toes to play in them because pieces of metal were exposed inside the boot. Angela never complained though. She was just happy to have her own skates. They represented her chance for the future she wanted so badly.

On most winter weekends, Angela would be on the ice all day, sometimes playing until close to midnight. Back then, her favourite person to play with was a man from Flemingdon Park who was famous around the neighbourhood both for his remarkable skill and for "grunting" while he played. Angela never spoke to this man or got his name. She believed he may have had a hearing disability. She loved the way he skated, and when they were on the ice together, she mimicked his every stride. Eventually, Angela even picked up his grunting habit—to the displeasure of many of her future opponents. If you were chasing the puck, and you heard that grunt coming from behind, you knew something bad was going to happen. At best, you'd lose the puck, at worst, you'd become part of the end boards thanks to a massive hit.

Once she was ready to call it a night, Angela would leave her skates on and walk from the rink through the large field lined with hydro towers that led to her home. In winter, the field would often freeze over with icy patches. Angela saw this as a good opportunity to continue to work on her skating, jumping from patch to patch to get a few more strides in. When she would eventually walk through the door with her boots and hockey stick in hand, Donna never asked any questions. She knew exactly where her youngest daughter had been. "Get some rest," Donna would always say. "You've got hockey in the morning."

CHAPTER 4

Playing With The Boys

Donna did everything she could to persuade Angela to pursue swimming. She went as far as registering Angela for lessons at the neighbourhood pool on weekends, hoping that her daughter would fall for the sport the same way she had for hockey. Angela enjoyed swimming and agreed to take the lessons to make her mother happy, but it wasn't long before she stopped going. As it turned out, the swimming lessons were interfering with hockey, and for Angela the choice between the two sports was no choice at all. When Donna found out about Angela's disappearing act, she wasn't happy. Donna knew her daughter was a talented hockey player, however, back then "no girl went anywhere in hockey."[1] It wasn't until a neighbour came up to Donna to rave about Angela's hockey ability that she realized her daughter may have a chance to do something special in the sport after all. From that day forward, Donna did everything she could to allow her daughter to play the game. The first challenge was finding her a league.

Up until she was eight, all of Angela's hockey experience consisted of pick-up street hockey and shinny games in Flemingdon Park. She had never competed in an organized league before, and there wasn't really anywhere for her to play in the neighbourhood—except for the Flemingdon Boys Hockey Association, but no girl had played there before.

When Donna approached the league administration about allowing Angela to play, she was immediately greeted with a "no." When she later threatened the president and his association with legal action, there was a quick change in policy.[2] Despite having no money to her name, Donna was prepared to bring the issue to the attention of the government as a human rights violation. Right from the time Angela was small, I ran into politics," recalls Donna. "That's hockey."

With Angela registered in an official league, the next challenge for Donna was to find her daughter all the necessary equipment. Like today, hockey wasn't cheap, and for a single mother raising five children, money was always in short supply. Somehow, Donna managed to scrape together what she needed to buy new and used equipment for Angela. "She had no money, but my mom would find a way to pay for things and get things done," says Angela. "For example, I remember every year we'd go to Wasaga Beach, and we didn't have a car. But every summer, we always got there. I don't know how she did it, but she always did. So I never went without equipment."

Up until Angela got her first part-time job as a teenager, Donna paid for all of her hockey equipment. "I wouldn't want my kids in hockey today," confesses Donna. "Even at that time $60 a year for house league was a lot of money. And you used to pay so much per week." Luckily for Donna's wallet, back then the kids didn't have to wear all the equipment that is required today. In her early playing days, Angela never wore a face mask or neck guard; a helmet and mouth piece were the only things that protected her from serious injury.

When Donna told her daughter she would be playing in the Flemingdon Boys Hockey Association, Angela was overflowing with excitement. The opportunity to play in an organized league was all Angela wanted. She knew she was the best street hockey player in the neighbourhood, and this was her opportunity to prove that she was the best ice hockey player, as well. So with her powder blue uniform and brand name Lange skates, Angela took to the ice wearing no. 11 and showed the league president that girls could play. In Angela's case, she did more than just play—she dominated.

In her first year, Angela was the leading scorer both on her team and in the league.[3] She started out at the lowest level, novice, but was later moved to atom and eventually peewee because she was such a scoring machine.[4] Nearly every time Angela touched the puck, it ended up in the back of the net. The only way anyone could stop her on the ice was to take her down, and when that happened, Angela didn't cry. She picked herself up, and gave it right back. "It was tough hockey," she says. "Guys tripped me and I remember two-handing them back."

Angela strikes a fierce pose in her Flemingdon Park uniform.
(Note the homemade "A" on the left shoulder.)

Angela's performance on the ice earned her the league scoring title and a selection to the league all-star team. She even represented the Flemingdon Boys Hockey Association at a peewee tournament in Montreal. Angela said that was a telling accomplishment for her. "That was pretty special to be chosen," she says. "I think I probably knew then that I could play."

When she started her second season, the no. 11 was taken and Angela had to select a new one. After some careful thought, she eventually settled on the no. 8, which she would go on to wear for the rest of her playing days. "I just thought you put no. 8 on its side and it's infinity," says Angela. "That's kind of how it went down."

In her second season, Angela was clearly the best player in the entire association. Donna, who watched all of Angela's games, said she easily outskated, outshot and outhit her male counterparts on every shift. Unfortunately for Angela, all of the other parents in the stands took notice and started questioning why a girl was playing in a boy's league. It wasn't long before the league president took notice, too. His son played on Angela's team and he was not happy a girl was outplaying his own boy. He searched out Donna after a game one night and delivered some bad news. "No girls can play anymore," he said.

"Why?" asked Donna.

"No, no, no…she'll have to go somewhere else," replied the president, never mentioning Angela by name.

"You are a male chauvinist pig," yelled Donna. "The only reason you don't want her in the league is because she is better than your son."

Angela never played another game in the Flemingdon Boys Hockey Association; the president saw to it that the league remained open only to boys. When Donna broke the news, Angela was devastated. She just wanted to play hockey, and at that moment her world came to an end. Donna saw how upset her daughter was and started to ask around about other leagues. That's when she heard about Annunciation, an all girl's hockey league run by the Catholic Church out of the Victoria Village Arena in North York. Donna immediately registered Angela, but she didn't get the reaction she thought she would from her daughter. "I was a little disappointed because when I first went there, there were all these girls in figure skates," recalls Angela. "And I was like, 'What is this? You shouldn't be wearing figure skates in hockey.'"

Because Annunciation was still in its formative years, there were other strange practices adopted by the league: namely, girls of all ages played together on the same team. The league simply didn't have enough players at that time to separate teams into proper age brackets, so seven-year-olds played on the same team as 14-year-olds.[5] The age differences among the players did little to alter Angela's game. Just like she did in the boy's league, she quickly emerged as the best player on the ice and advanced to the more competitive Lower Lakes Girls Hockey League, playing with a team from the Grandravine neighbourhood of Toronto.

Even when she played with girls, unfortunately, Angela still had to deal with racism. Kym, who never missed any of her younger sister's practices or games when they were growing up, said the racial taunts followed Angela to every arena she played in. "It happened quite a bit," she says. "When people would say nasty things about her colour, I didn't understand it. There was no black and white for us, so I never looked at Angela any different because that's how our mother raised us." On one occasion Kym remembers a father on an opposing team becoming enraged with Angela after she knocked down his daughter in a battle for the puck. The middle-aged man stood up in his seat and yelled, "No little nigger is going to hit my daughter." Kym, of course, heard this and marched right up to his face to set him straight. "Who the hell do you think you are calling my sister a nigger?" she said. "She is not your sister!" he replied. "Yes, she is!"

The racial taunts did little to impact Angela's game. She eventually skipped bantam and entered right into Ladies Senior C with the Newtonbrook Saints, when she was just 13.[6] Looking, back, Angela describes it as "craziness" that a 13-year-old would be playing full contact hockey against women 16 and over. At the time, though, she just wanted to play. She had more than outgrown the Lower Lakes Girls Hockey League and was itching to test her skills against players of similar calibre, even if it meant playing against women twice her age. Senior hockey was her only long-term option.

"I'd just sit in the dressing room and see all these older girls and I just knew I was putting on my skates and going out to play," she says.

"Because I knew I could play, I didn't really worry so much about people beside me." Angela was blazing a trail never experienced before in girls' hockey. From early on it was clear to all who watched her that she was headed for greatness. Off the ice, however, was a whole other story.

Even with all her early hockey success, Angela was still getting into trouble in the Park. Friends constantly exposed her to drugs and alcohol, and she couldn't seem to avoid getting into fights. It was all she could do to keep her focus on hockey. Part of the reason for Angela's problems had to do with her lack of interest in school. The only regular class Angela ever attended was gym; she spent the rest of her time devising schemes to get out of school, including setting off the buildings' fire alarm. By the time she entered Valley Park Middle School, Angela was close to becoming another drop-out statistic. But her fate changed when she met a caring vice principal named Ross Dixon. Mr. Dixon took an immediate liking to Angela, getting to know her during her many visits to the principal's office. For the next three years, this strict disciplinarian took Angela under his wing and showed her learning could be both fun and rewarding. To this day, Angela credits the late vice principal for keeping her in school, as well as for her love of Greek mythology. "He stepped out of his role as vice principal to teach me," remembers Angela. "From that point on I started getting into my studies—a little bit."

Thanks to Mr. Dixon's guidance, Angela went on to Overlea High School and, eventually, into post-secondary school. A number of Angela's friends weren't so lucky. The drugs and alcohol they experimented with as kids became chronic problems for many of them. Some died, a few were incarcerated and others just disappeared. It was clear that Flemingdon Park was changing for the worse, and Donna desperately wanted to move her family into a better neighbourhood. By the time she entered her teens, Angela, too, was ready to leave the Park behind, and her ticket out was sports.

CHAPTER 5

College Star

As Angela entered her teens, she was wondering about her sexuality and trying to balance the many positive and negative influences to which she was exposed. "I was a bit of a rebel at the time," says Angela. "Lots of stuff is coming at you. You have your home life and your neighbourhood life, then you have your school life. Drugs are there, alcohol is there. At that time, guys—you get a special feeling for guys. And then it's like, 'well is it guys or is it girls?'"

Angela was coming to the realization that physically and emotionally she was strongly attracted to females. At the time, she was concerned what people might think, especially her family. For her sisters it was not an issue, and when Angela told her mom that she was a lesbian, Donna said to her, "You are my daughter. I don't like it. But I will accept it." At such a young age, Angela didn't trumpet this news to the world. High school kids can be cruel, and for Angela, her private life was best kept private—a feeling that would remain into her adulthood. Her sexuality was neither something to be ashamed of, nor did she make it a political issue. It was her business and no one else's.

With the changes she was experiencing, she was lucky to have a group of friends with which she could be herself and find comfort and support. She began going to parties and, eventually, to clubs in downtown Toronto, which was for her both an eye opener and a relief. "I remember thinking, 'Oh wow. I am not the only one. There are others,'" says Angela. "So I stayed within those circles. I was not ridiculed or made fun of because I was around other gay people."

As if these personal discoveries weren't enough for her to handle, when Angela was 14 and about to enter Grade 10 at Overlea High School, her mother announced they were moving. Angela was completely shocked by the news because she knew her mother couldn't afford to live anywhere else. By this time, all three girls were regularly pitching in with the rent and utility bills to avoid eviction and keep the lights on. Angela had started working as a busgirl at a downtown Toronto steakhouse. As part of the job, she had to wear nylons and a dress, which always gave the family a good chuckle, seeing their tomboy dressed up like a little lady. So Angela thought it was a practical joke when her mother said their days of living in government housing were over. But it was no joke. Donna had received an unexpected inheritance cheque and put it toward first and last month's rent on an apartment unit at Graydon Hall, located 15 minutes up the street from Flemingdon Park.

When Donna delivered the news to Angela, she expected some resistance. It had long been her dream to move her family out of government housing, but she knew how much Angela loved living in the Park. To Donna's surprise, Angela embraced the change. "It seemed kind of neat at the time," says Angela. "I was at a different stage at that point, a bit more mature, and I knew I couldn't do what I did there as a kid." Donna, Kym and Angela happily packed their bags and moved to their new home. Cindy, meanwhile, moved in with her boyfriend, Gary, who she would soon marry. It appeared things were finally going well for Donna and her girls.

Over at her new school, Georges Vanier Secondary School, Angela picked up where she left off on the sports front. Just a few blocks up the street at Seneca College, word quickly spread about a young female hockey and softball star who was dominating the competition. The timing for the college could not have been more perfect; they already had a women's hockey program and were laying the groundwork to start a softball team. Mary Zettel, one of the architects of the softball program, coveted an athlete with Angela's skills and envisioned her in a Seneca Scouts uniform. Over the course of two years, she struck up a friendship with the young star, attending her games and providing her with information about Seneca's programs and sports opportunities.

Until meeting Mary, Angela had no plans of attending college after high school. She had struggled with school work her entire childhood and planned to continue bussing tables once she graduated. Despite her athletic gifts, there wasn't a professional women's hockey or softball league where she could earn a living. "I remembered saying, 'When I get older, I hope to get a good job and make $10 an hour," says Angela. "That was the goal."

As she entered her final year of high school, at Mary's insistence, Angela decided to apply to college. To Mary's delight, Seneca was her first choice. Angela chose the Recreation Facilities Management diploma program, which was the same program Mary graduated from in 1977. At the time, Angela only cared about playing sports at the varsity level and never gave much thought to what she would be studying or if she'd find a job after graduation. Mary seemed happy with the program, and that was enough for Angela to feel it would be a good fit for her as well. A few months after applying, she received a letter from Seneca saying she had been accepted. This was a monumental achievement for the same girl who, years earlier, would always ditch classes and never do any homework. Unfortunately, what should have been a time of celebration for Angela was overshadowed by more family drama.

The family's fresh start at Graydon Hall had quickly turned into a horrible nightmare when Donna lost her hotel job. To make matters worse, she had fallen behind on the rent and all the inheritance money she had received was spent. Donna didn't have the heart to tell her girls the financial state the family was in. Instead, they found out the hard way when they arrived home one night to discover a huge padlock on the door. The landlord had locked them out. Cindy, who was now living on her own, offered to take in her mother and sisters at the apartment she shared with Gary. Angela accepted, while Kym opted to go it alone on the streets, still struggling to cope with the horrible abuse she had endured as a child. Donna suffered another nervous breakdown and required treatment. Like she had done hundreds of times before, Angela threw herself into hockey and softball to take her mind off her family's troubles. "Thank God for sports," she says. "That was my way out."

In the fall of 1981, Angela donned her familiar no. 8 jersey for the

Seneca Scouts women's softball team for the first time. Up until this point, everyone knew Angela could play hockey, but very few people knew about her standout skills on the diamond. Linda Stapleton, now Seneca's Director of Athletics, was an assistant coach on the team and said Angela wasted no time asserting her dominance in the Ontario Colleges Athletic Association (OCAA). In a game against Loyalist College, Linda recalls Angela hitting the ball so far into a cornfield that it never returned. "I was amazed by her strength," says Linda, who is now one of Angela's best friends and colleagues. "She had a powerful throwing arm as well—just a super athlete.

Angela could play any position on the diamond, but was mostly an outfielder for the Scouts. She hit clean up, and thanks to her bat, Seneca won the inaugural OCAA Championship. Angela was named a league all-star, and in subsequent seasons led the Scouts to another OCAA gold and silver medal. Yet it was on the ice where she set herself apart.

Up until the college level, Angela always played centre. That all changed when she met Lee Trempe, the head coach of the Seneca Scouts. Lee was a respected and "no nonsense" coach from the Central Ontario Women's Hockey League (COWHL). She had been the bench boss of the Scouts for two seasons before Angela joined the team in 1982. The pair had known each other from senior hockey. Lee invited Angela to play for her team, but she had politely declined. When they met again at Seneca there were no hard feelings—just a lot of optimism for the upcoming season. With the addition of Angela, the Scouts immediately went from a good team to OCAA gold medal contenders. To ensure that goal became reality, Lee decided to move Angela back to defence. "With her talent and ability, it made sense to give her more ice to work with, as opposed to cutting it down on her," says Lee. "She was able to setup plays, get the puck out of our own end and incorporate the rest of the players into whatever system we were using."

Double Threat: Angela the college softball star.

Angela accepted her new assignment and it worked very well for her, not to mention the Scouts. Just like Lee had predicted, Angela was able to see the entire ice like never before. More importantly, the move did little to hurt her offence. In fact, in her first season with the Scouts, Angela led the team and the league in scoring with 25 points in eight games (15 goals, 10 assists). The Scouts went on to win the silver medal that season, and Angela claimed her first OCAA women's hockey most valuable player award. Not bad for a 16-year-old straight out of high school. "She was the best," says Lee. "There wasn't anything she couldn't do on the ice." The only problem was that Angela's mastery on skates didn't exactly follow her into the classroom.

In her first year as a college student, Angela found herself on thin ice academically. Now, it wasn't because she wasn't smart enough. Angela admits she never made the time to study or finish her homework. In her defence, during college, Angela not only played for the varsity softball and hockey teams, she also played both sports in competitive leagues outside of school. In addition, she held numerous part-time jobs—from bussing tables at two restaurants to working the snack bar at the Seneca arena as well as refereeing games. Angela's poor grades became an issue with the College's administrators, who threatened to sit her out if she didn't get her act together. Linda recalls hearing Lee tell Angela, "If you want to play and you want to stick around with the team, you have to focus on your academics. You are not here just to be a hockey player. You are here to graduate."

Linda and Lee both strongly believe a large part of Angela's academic struggles that first year had a lot to do with her attitude and the free reign she enjoyed as child and teenager growing up in Flemingdon Park. She was never really disciplined or held accountable for her actions. That attitude didn't fly with Lee, who was a disciplinarian by nature and took it upon herself to drive home the importance of getting an education, nor with Linda. After many heated discussions, Lee said Angela finally realized that "if you want to get ahead in life you had to get an education." So Angela settled down and began to apply herself. With the help of the college's tutors and her coach she made it through her first year of post-secondary education. No one was happier for her than Lee, who had quickly become a mother figure to Angela. "I really looked up to her," says Angela. "She would always talk to me in terms of what I was doing with my life, making sure I was going in the right direction. I don't think you will find anybody that wouldn't say Lee was a great person and coach."

On the home front, things were getting better for Angela's mother. Donna was back on her feet again and had found a place to sublet close to the college thanks to a connection of Cindy's. It wasn't long before Angela moved back in with her mother, and the two became closer than ever. Happily for everyone, Donna's Graydon Hall breakdown would be her last.

Entering her second season with the Scouts, Angela was named captain. She was optimistic about the team's chances on the ice, as they were all a year older and the disappointment of not winning the OCAA gold medal had given the team a clear focus for the 1983–84 season. Angela had gained a reputation around the league and became a target for opponents. She was bigger and stronger in her second year and driven to live up to her hype. That season, the team's fan base grew and people were coming out from club teams and men's hockey to watch Angela in action. To her delight, Donna, too, had become a regular fixture at the arena. She got a job at a gas station and was working at the college's residence. After her shift ended, she would make her way over to the Seneca College Sports Centre. "It was strange watching her play defence," says Donna. "But she could play any position."

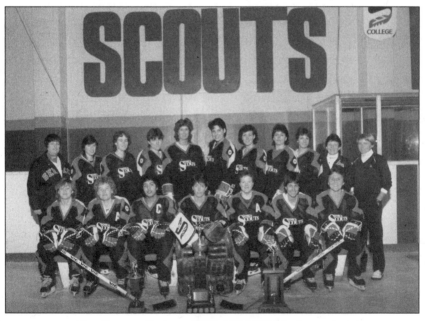

The Seneca Scouts, 1983-1984 OCAA champions.
Angela's coach and mentor Lee Trempe is at back left.

In her sophomore year, Angela scored 15 goals again, with 30 points in 10 games played. The only way her opponents could stop her was to take her down, but that just got her angry and made her even tougher to play against. "Quite frankly, she was a force to be reckoned with," says Lee. "She was a very difficult player to try to stop. She was strong physically. Her skating ability was the best. And when she wound up to take a slap shot, you never wanted to be in front of it. It was probably the first and last time you would." Angela led the Scouts to their first championship that season. She once again won the scoring title and was named the OCAA most valuable player. What came next, in her final season, would forever seal her legacy as Ontario's, and arguably Canada's, greatest college athlete.

Scoring 50 goals in a team's first 50 games of the season is a difficult task, even for the world's most talented hockey players. In the NHL it has only been achieved eight times. Wayne Gretzky accomplished this feat faster than any other professional hockey player by scoring 50 goals in 39 games. In her final season with the Scouts, Angela hit that magic number of 50 goals in just 14 games played, adding 23 assists for 73 points. What magnifies this accomplishment even further, however, is when you take into consideration that Angela was playing defence. It was then that a local reporter who chronicled Angela's record-breaking season dubbed her "the Wayne Gretzky of women's hockey."

For Angela, the icing on the cake that season was another gold medal, which complimented her third scoring title and most valuable player honour. To this day, she still holds the OCAA record for most goals in a season and is the league's all-time leading scorer.[1]

In the spring of 1985, Angela graduated from Seneca and Linda hired her full-time as a sports programmer. Although she was no longer eligible to play at the varsity level, Angela moved behind the bench as an assistant coach, and with Lee's direction, the pair led the Scouts to yet another championship. The following season, Lee moved on and Angela became the head coach. She accepted the job for one season and delivered a fourth straight title.

This time, a large part of the credit had to go to another up and coming blueliner named Geraldine Heaney. Geraldine had come to Canada from Ireland and was playing in the COWHL for the North York Aeros. Just like Angela, she had been recruited to the Seneca Scouts and enrolled in the Recreation Facilities Management program. Angela and Geraldine became fast friends and would eventually become inseparable.

Sadly, in 1989, the OCAA women's hockey league folded due to a lack of participating teams. Although the news greatly upset Angela, by that time, there were lots of opportunities for young women like her to develop their skills at the club level and, eventually, in the service of their country.

CHAPTER 6

Mastering Her Craft
(With Snot All Over Her Itec)

The Central Ontario Women's Hockey League (COWHL) was founded in 1980 and provided the highest level of competition for women hockey players in Ontario. The league would harvest many future Canadian national team members, including Cathy Phillips, Geraldine Heaney, Cassie Campbell-Pascall, Cheryl Pounder and Marianne Grnak. Angela's impact on the COWHL would be immense. She would lead the league in scoring from 1987 through 1994, and again in 1996; she was an all-star for three consecutive seasons and league MVP six times; and she was selected as MVP in the national championships an unprecedented eight times. Yet, with all these accolades to her credit, Angela doesn't feel the need to characterize her career based on accomplishment. To her, it went by in a furious "blur" of fun, growth and friendship. It is easier for her to recall the people she met and the times they shared, as opposed to the many games she dominated

Angela's 18-year career in the COWHL began with the Toronto Islanders when she was 14 years old. She was just a skinny kid who had yet to fill into the rock solid, 170-pound frame that would eventually be used to paste countless opponents into the boards with her trademark bone-crunching hits. For now, however, it was Angela who would have to take her lumps. The COWHL was the best league in Ontario, and it was also the toughest. "There wasn't the great development stream, which kind of makes it incredible that Angela got to the height that she did," says CBC sports analyst Robin Brown, who also played in the COWHL. "From midget to senior, there was nothing in between. You either sank or swam. Many of the girls didn't make the team right off and stopped playing."

With her swagger, talent and fearlessness, Angela became an instant target. Like when she'd fight older, stronger boys in the fields of Flemingdon Park, she never shied from the centre of the action. In fact, she loved it. "She took care of herself," says Donna. "If someone checked her really bad, I'd say, 'Watch out for no. 8!' But in a lot of ways I was nervous about her playing." Although Donna knew "no. 8" could handle herself on the ice, she made a point of finding one of the older girls on the team to watch out for her young daughter. With the Saints, Angela had Carol Law looking out for her, and when she moved to the Islanders, a teammate named Anne Michaeljohn took her under her wing.

Watching her on the ice, one would not think Angela to be out of her element. "She was very strong on her skates and had a really dynamic bullet-like shot," remembers woman's hockey historian and author Elizabeth Etue. "I don't think many people were as strong or as fast, which is why she dominated from such a young age."

Yet the social aspect of playing on a team full of adults takes some getting used to for an impressionable 15-year-old. Angela kept to herself and let her play speak for itself. But, like anyone, she just wanted to be one of the girls. This is not easy to do when you are dependent on others for rides and the social activity of choice is a post game trip to the bar. "You just want to go and have fun and hang out, but you don't really have the resources to do that," says Angela. "Afterwards, if they were to go out for a beer, well, you know what? I was going out for a beer too. I started quite young with that aspect of things, probably too young."

Angela's relationships with her teammates were built and nurtured on and off the ice during road trips across Ontario's "Golden Horseshoe." The Islanders played in towns and cities like Agincourt, North York, Toronto, Mississauga, Brampton, Burlington and Hamilton. Having played hockey for so long, many of Angela's experiences blur together. She doesn't remember how she got to many of her games, but she always found a way. At first she didn't have a car, because she was too young to drive. Friends, family and teammates would pick her up, making sure the teenage phenom got to the rink on time.

The Islanders folded in 1982, as was often the case with COWHL teams. Angela then ventured even further from home, joining Burlington's team, nicknamed "Mark's Diesels" after the team's sponsor Mark Burrell (Mark fixed diesel trucks for a living, so the name was a no brainer). Angela was recruited to Burlington by Bob Phillips, father of the star goaltender, Cathy Phillips. Bob was a dedicated volunteer and a long-time coach for Burlington and Hamilton. He was behind the bench as Cathy established herself as one of Canada's greatest female goaltenders. She played 17 seasons in the COWHL, was voted MVP twice and top goaltender 14 times. She would also go on to backstop Canada to its first world championship in 1990 and participate in seven Canadian championships before a benign brain tumour ended her career. As two of the premier players in the league, Angela and Cathy developed a friendly rivalry as competitors and a lifelong friendship as teammates. "We had a mutual respect for each other," says Cathy. "I knew I had to play my 'A' game against her, and so did she. I remember Angela said, 'You know, I kind of prefer playing against you because it's more of a challenge.' That's how I felt too."

The star of "Mark's Diesels" awaits the puck drop in Burlington.

When Cathy's father showed up at Angela's doorstep in his Winnebago and asked her to play for him, she had no idea how far she'd have to travel to get to games. It was an hour each way from her home in North York, and Angela was also trying to balance school and her part-time jobs. Things got a little easier when she got her first car. With the help of her father, she scraped together $600 to buy a used Chevy Nova. When it died, Angela bought a Dodge Omni, until the bottom fell out when she took a corner a little too tightly.

Transportation issues aside, Angela stayed in Burlington for three years, from 1981, through 1984. Her time there included her first experience in a Canadian senior women's championship, held in Brantford, Ontario. In 1983, Burlington won the second-ever Abby Hoffman Cup as the top women's hockey team in Canada. This would be the first of 12 appearances in the nationals for Angela—experiences that have remained some of her favourite in hockey. "The nationals were awesome," says Angela. "We had great crowds all the time for those. It was an opportunity for every province to come together and play. It was definitely great hockey. I used to love it."

With the tight competition on the ice during these championships came the camaraderie off it. At the time, the national championships took place in a different province each year. They would run from Wednesday through Sunday, with entertainment, theme nights and dinners. Players would enjoy themselves, swimming at the hotel and getting to know colleagues from all over Canada. With lots of hockey to play, they were sure to make curfew—at least until Sunday night. "On Sunday, everybody drank," recalls Angela.

The nationals would become an annual event for Angela, even if her COWHL team did not make it out of the provincials. The province's best team had the option to "pick up" other players from their province to bolster its roster for the Canadian championship, and Angela was always at the top of that list. After three years in Burlington, Angela joined the Agincourt Canadians for the 1984–85 season. She chose Agincourt because her mentor and college coach,

Lee Trempe, was behind the bench. It was not the right fit for Lee or Angela, and both departed after one season. Angela remembers it as a "strange" year. She was in her final year of college at Seneca, and her time and energy were being split between the Canadians and the Scouts.

In 1985, Angela joined the Brampton Canadettes for one season, where she played with Fran Rider, one of the most dedicated volunteers in the history of women's hockey. Fran has given more than 30 years to the game as a player, administrator, board member and president of the Ontario Woman's Hockey Association (OWHA). She had followed Angela's career closely, first becoming aware of her as a 12-year-old standout in the Lower Lakes league. "We were always looking to find her places to play," says Fran.

After years of playing defence against Angela, Fran was thrilled to finally be on the same side of the ice. Although, like Cathy, she loved the challenge of trying to stop her, Fran realized the impact of having Angela's talent on her team: "You always knew, in any game you were in, if Angela was on your hockey team, you had a solid chance to win," says Fran. "Some days, when you were down a goal, or a couple of goals, you'd look down the bench and see that no. 8: 'Okay, now's the time, Angela.'"

Although Angela's stay in Brampton was a short one, she remembers it fondly. The team travelled to tournaments in Quebec and had some outstanding players, including Colleen Cohen, Sue Harley, Tracy Horton and Leslie Hood. They received good media coverage in Brampton and enjoyed a small but loyal fan base of players' families and friends. For Angela's teammates, even their practices took on extra importance with her around. They'd marvel at the work ethic and intensity that accompanied her abilities. "Every time she would go on the ice, you would see another move," remembers Fran. "It was a treat to watch. You'd get caught up watching her and have to give yourself a shake and get back into position."

Angela's next stop was with the Mississauga Warriors for the 1986–87 season. Again, Angela followed Lee Trempe there. She would stay in Mississauga for three seasons, largely due to feeling comfortable with the personnel and leadership. As much as Angela wanted to win, she wanted even more to enjoy playing and to build relationships with her teammates and coaches. "I had a really good time in Mississauga," says Angela. "It had to do with the organization and the direction they were going. The staff that they had really influenced how I felt."

Angela's first season in Mississauga was also the year of the first-ever world tournament in women's hockey. Although not sanctioned by the International Ice Hockey Federation, women's teams from all around the world, including Japan, Sweden, the United States, Switzerland and Holland, came to Ontario to compete against one another for the first time. West Germany, originally a strong advocate for international competition, withdrew its team because of Canada's decision to remove intentional bodychecking from the women's game in 1986. Instead, the West Germans sent a representative to observe, as did four other countries. The tournament was administered by the OWHA, with Fran Rider front and centre. Fran referred to the 1987 tournament as her greatest accomplishment and "the key event in the history of international women's hockey."[1]

"We worked aggressively to secure the world tournament," says Fran. "We had Mississauga Mayor Hazel McCallion as our honorary chair. I remember Marian Coveny, who was the team captain for Team Canada, when she stepped on the ice for the first game, saying 'This is a giant step for women kind.'" At this tournament, Team Canada was represented by the winner of the Canadian national championship. In 1987, the Hamilton Golden Hawks were Canada's best team, thanks in large part to picking up Angela from Mississauga for the nationals.

Fresh off the first of her seven consecutive COWHL scoring titles, Angela was released by Lee to play with Hamilton as they took on

Canada's best teams for the right to represent the country internationally. However, when the world tournament came around, the OWHA also decided to include a second Canadian team, dubbed "Team Ontario." This team would help to strengthen the competition in what was an uneven international field. It was decided Team Ontario would be the number two team in the COWHL, which happened to be Angela's regular team, the Mississauga Warriors. Naturally, the Warriors wanted to have their elite player on the ice when they faced the best in the world. Angela entered the tournament with mixed emotions. "Lee had released me to go play with Hamilton at the nationals that year," says Angela. "I was really instrumental in winning that championship. Then to come back and say that I had to go back to my other team [Mississauga], I really didn't think it was fair. But I had pressure from my coach, who said, 'You're playing here.'"

As the main representatives for Canada, Hamilton was able to go around the country to pick up the country's best players, including Colleen Cohen from Ontario, Shirley Cameron and Dawn McGuire from Alberta and Donna Ladassure from Saskatchewan. This put the icing on what was, essentially, Canada's first modern-day all-star women's hockey team. "It was so nice to see them have that opportunity, it was a dream come true for them," says Fran.

In the tournament's first round "Team Canada" beat Switzerland 10–0, Sweden 8–2, Japan 11–0 and Holland 19–0. The game against the United States was a closer contest, with Canada winning 2–1, while Angela's Team Ontario lost 5–0 to the Americans. Ontario would rebound to beat the Americans 5–2 in the semi-final, setting up an all-COWHL final: Angela and her Team Ontario Warriors against the Team Canada she had led to the national championship and the right to represent Canada.

Cathy Phillips backstopped Canada to a 4–0 shutout in the final. Cathy was the difference in the game, making some spectacular saves, including stopping Angela on a breakaway. Despite the loss, and the bitter feeling of being forced off of Team Canada, Angela learned a great deal at the 1987 tournament. It was her first exposure to international competition—experience that would serve her well in the coming years.

From a global perspective, the tournament was a big step forward for women's hockey. For the first time, the world's greatest players were on display in one location, and they did not disappoint. The competition was uneven, with the North American teams at a distinct advantage over the European and Asian teams, but the women involved showed they could play technically sound, fiery, exciting hockey. Although media attention was "paltry,"[2] the tournament was a key bargaining chip in the effort to convince the IIHF to sanction a world championship for women's hockey. "It was very exciting. We got some respect," says Cathy. "It showed that we could play hockey. We didn't get a lot of media attention, but we sure got more than we usually do. That was huge for us. And Fran Rider was smart enough to invite the IIHF, and they saw the competition was good. If it wasn't for that, we'd still be playing in the background."

Back in the COWHL, and now with international experience under her belt, Angela continued to improve her game with Mississauga and cement her reputation as the most dangerous player in the league. As with the NHL's Original Six—or any league with a small number of teams—rivalries grew strong as teams played each other often. Players would come to know one another well, challenging each other to elevate their games—as was the case with Angela and Cathy and the league's other top players. Some bad blood was inevitable.

Angela remembers many an on-ice war with her friend from Seneca and future teammate Geraldine Heaney. Though the pair would eventually make a formidable duo for Team Canada, they began as COWHL adversaries. Often referred to as "the Bobby Orr of women's hockey," Geraldine would spend 18 years playing senior hockey, all with the Toronto Aeros. She began playing in the COWHL when she was just 13, was part of six provincial championship teams, and participated in every national championship from 1987 to 2001. "We used to kill each other," says Angela. "She was with the Aeros and I was with Mississauga. You always knew she was always going to make great decisions and great plays."

Angela also recalls Linda DeAngelis, a player with Hamilton who also "used to kill her all the time." Though today most players use metal cage masks, at that time, players used clear plastic face shields they called "Itecs" after the company that made them. After coming out of the corner with Linda, Angela says she would have "snot all over her Itec" thanks to her vicious hits. "Angela did take a certain amount of abuse. She was a target because she was the best," says Fran. "And that made her even better because everybody is at the top of their game when they face her, and she kept pushing her game to the next level."

It is often overlooked by hockey historians that senior women's hockey was very tough, and hitting was an integral part of competition until 1986. That year, the Canadian Amateur Hockey Association decided that it was hazardous to many players who had not been trained to properly give and receive hits, so hitting was banned. Yet the women's game remained physical, in contrast to the assumption that female players were not interested in a grinding, tough style of play. Angela was one of the players who helped to erase this false assumption. "Girls' hockey was criticized for players not having enough strength," says Robin Brown, a former Brampton Canadettes. "Angela wasn't like that. She was a really good bodychecker. Hitting her was like hitting steel. She was very solid. I liked the bodychecking part of the game too. And we'd meet on the ice once and while."

Twenty years later, left winger Judy Butler, another veteran of the COWHL who also played against Angela while at York University, remembers quite clearly the toll playing against Angela took on her body: "She was solid. All around solid," says Judy. "I'd try to stay out of her way. I definitely feel the hits to this day, to be honest with you."

After three years with Mississauga, Angela was recruited to join Geraldine Heaney on what had become the best team in the COWHL—the Toronto Aeros. With Angela's relatively short stops in Burlington, Agincourt, Brampton and Mississauga, Robin Brown remembers how it had become a running joke around the league: "What team will Angela be with this year? Who will be our toughest competition?" Angela concedes that she was approached to play on many teams throughout her career. Though there was no money to be made for players at that time, being the hottest commodity in the COWHL was a nice position to be in for Angela: it provided the freedom to join the best programs and play with those she respected as players and friends.

With the Aeros, Angela finally felt as though she could "settle down" and foresee a future with one team. She appreciated the quality of the coaching and was excited by the prospect of learning more and taking her game to another level. "It was just a matter of time before you broke down and went to the Aeros," says Angela. "Even today, they are still the number one organization, as far as I am concerned."

The Aeros were an ideal fit for Angela, not only because it was a case of the best player going to the best team, but because joining them brought her full circle: the team was formed in 1974, out of the old Annunciation team where Angela got her start playing organized girls hockey. Formed by players' parents, the motto for the Aeros was for its players "to enjoy playing a competitive sport, to develop elite hockey skills and good life skills that would take them to leadership roles in the future."

The Aeros put this philosophy into practice by employing coaches who understood the technical side of the game and could teach it to women the same way it had been imparted to male hockey players. In Canada, talented male hockey players have the benefit of world-class instruction from the first time they lace up their skates. Girls like Angela, growing up in the mid-1970s, were not so fortunate. The outstanding systems in place for Canadian female players today were not even imagined, and Angela had only the limited knowledge of well-meaning volunteers and parents.

Instead, she learned through observation—watching older players, male and female, emulating their actions and using her own skill to build on what she saw. This began with her first role model, the smooth skating man in Flemingdon Park, and continued throughout her time in the COWHL. With the Aeros, Angela was exposed to the technical coaching that she needed to complement her natural abilities. She became part of a more systematic approach, learning to play as part of a five-player unit and incorporating "special teams" strategies for power plays and penalty kills. The style of play in the COWHL was becoming more and more sophisticated, and teams like the Aeros were ahead of the curve in teaching the skills and team play that would eventually become the foundation of the Canadian national program.

Ever the observant hockey student, Angela was open to improving her understanding of the game. Coaches like Lee Trempe had served as mentors, guiding Angela through her teens and helping her make the decisions that kept her out of trouble and furthered her career. Now, at age 25, she was at the apex of her talent and needed another kind of guidance. The Aeros had just the man for the job.

"You learn something from all your coaches, whether it's something about yourself or something about people or something about the game," says Angela. "Technically, the best coach I had growing up was Ken Dufton." Ken was a veteran of 10 years coaching male hockey at the junior level. He and the Aeros' owner and manager, Colin MacKenzie, wanted to approach women's hockey the same way men's junior hockey functioned in Ontario. This meant facilitating success by providing their players with the resources they needed: more practice time, better equipment, sponsorship and a strategy for winning. "Ken would go out of his way to be up-to-date as to what's going on in the game technically, and he does a lot of work before practices, a lot of prep work," says Angela. "I've done a lot of coaching courses since playing for him, so I know what he was doing was right."

Ken had coached the Aeros since 1987, and he was well aware of Angela and her skills when she arrived in 1989. The following year, she led the Aeros to their first national championship, scoring the winning goal in the 1–0 championship game against future Team Canada teammate Manon Rheaume. The Aeros would win another national championship two years later, a year in which Angela would score 40 goals in 28 games, while adding 30 assists for 70 points—an average of 2.5 points per game. In Wayne Gretzky's best seasons, he averaged 2.7 points per game.

"Well, Angela at her best was the most dominant player in the world at that time," says Ken. "She had what I call the 'wow' factor. There are a lot of good hockey players, a lot of great hockey players, but very few have the 'wow' factor. Alexander Ovechkin has it, Sidney Crosby has it. Angela had the 'wow' factor." With all that talent also came a desire to win and a temper that would sometimes get the better of Angela; Ken recalls that she already had a reputation around the league and was a target of other players because of her extraordinary talent, passion and competitiveness.

Her opponents knew that making Angela angry might throw her off her game, but it also might give her the motivation she needed to raise her game a notch and be the difference maker. Ken came to realize it was a fine line with Angela. "Angela played with a lot of passion. And sometimes the passion got the better of her," says Ken. "She is a very competitive person—extremely competitive. And in fairness to her, she was the subject of a lot of attention by opposition players. But at the same time, she gave much better than she ever took."

Under Ken's guidance, Angela was able to harness her natural gifts and learn how to play as part of a unit. She began to understand that it didn't always have to be an end-to-end rush and she could depend on her teammates to set her up for goals, instead of always being the playmaker herself. "Angela was a very dominant individual player," says Ken. "It was trying to find a better balance as to when to use her individual skills and when to move up and down the ice as part of five players." Ken saw greatness in Angela and tried to make her a more complete player by imparting his knowledge about the technical side of the game. Making Angela a part of a system was meant to improve her overall game, but it was impossible to overlook how special a player she was becoming. Although she had been a gifted scorer and playmaker from the time she was a child, Angela also possessed a physical stature that hockey players dream about.

With her strength, wide-legged skating style and low centre of gravity, Angela was nearly impossible to move off the puck or off her feet. CBC hockey analyst Scott Russell likened her to "a huge cat on the prowl," who could "generate explosive momentum in an instant."[3] Elizabeth Etue gave her the nickname "Freight Train" for her incredible drive and speed going up and down the ice. Ken remembers her as a very strong skater with a tremendous shot, who could beat defenders in different ways, burning them from the outside with her speed or from in close with her soft hands. "She was strong, like Mark Messier. She had the finesse of Wayne Gretzky," says Robin Brown. "She had some nice tricks with her stick handling. She could dominate with her physicality too. And she could hit. She had the whole package."

For Angela it was simply a matter of putting her talent and skill toward the only goal that mattered to her: winning. She knew what she could do on the ice and was confident in her ability. Yet, her constant desire to be the best is what really set Angela apart from all the other players in the COWHL, and, as it would turn out, players from around the world. While many gifted athletes can become complacent, her desire to win was unparalleled and undying.

"Well that's the whole reason you play, to compete," says Angela. "I think it's no different than Michael Jackson or Diana Ross with a microphone—that when they give you the microphone, don't ever give it back. With me and sport, if someone is trying to take a piece of me or take the puck away, you just keep fighting for what's yours and you don't give it up."

While taking her play in the COWHL to unprecedented levels, Angela would be presented a new challenge—to take her microphone onto the global stage and test herself against the best in the world. She would not disappoint.

Coming in second with Team Ontario during the first international tournament in 1987.

CHAPTER 7

On Top of the World

By 1990, Angela was widely considered the best player in Ontario and learning more about herself and her game. She was a 25-year-old college graduate with an outstanding college and club resume to her credit. She was working at Seneca College, bringing in some decent money, and realizing the life she wanted for herself. With her job, she could even afford to order her own sticks—Sherwood model 70-90, medium curve—with "James" stamped on them.

As she continued to win scoring titles and championships in the COWHL, a new challenge awaited her, thanks to the seeds that had been planted back in 1987 at the first international women's hockey tournament. Many players and volunteers had dreamed about an IIHF–sanctioned world hockey championship for women, including Fran Rider, who had been fighting the uphill battle for global exposure for the women's game for years. "When we were moving towards the world tournament, we were told very clearly by many, 'There will never be a world championship in your lifetime and women's hockey will never be in the Olympics,'" says Fran. "Yet the impossible dream was realized because women hockey enthusiasts from all countries came together in a cooperative atmosphere to make the competitive game better. That message was so powerful."

From the IIHF's perspective, the level of competition in North America was not an issue. The number of women playing on competitive club teams and in university and college programs had continued to grow. In Canada alone, 7,500 women were registered with the Canadian Amateur Hockey Association (CAHA), and an estimated 15,000 were playing the game across the country. To put those numbers into perspective, European countries were each seeing less than 1,000 females taking to the ice [1],making the talent pools across the Atlantic substantially smaller.

Yet after attending the 1989 Women's European Ice Hockey Championship, Dr. Günther Sabetzki of the IIHF determined that the calibre of play was high enough to support Canada's bid for a world championship. Canada would host this groundbreaking event, with games taking place in Ottawa, Ontario. Teams invited to compete were Finland, Sweden, Norway, Switzerland, West Germany, the U.S.A., Japan and Canada. Although it had been removed from the Canadian game, bodychecking would be allowed in international play. One could only imagine the sly smile that appeared on the face of a certain no. 8 when she heard that news.

With the realization of a world championship, the next task was to choose the very first Team Canada. The problem was nobody knew how to do it. The initial player screening was done by the provinces—all with different approaches—and the final roster was to be selected by the CAHA after a training camp in Mississauga. Dave McMaster, the late head coach of the University of Toronto's Lady Blues varsity hockey team, was chosen to lead the squad. He had previously coached the Hamilton Golden Hawks in the 1987 international tournament. "This was the first of anything at that level, so nobody knew what to expect and nobody knew this was how they did it or didn't do it because we had nothing to compare," says Angela. "And the CAHA were learning about the girls' game too."

Women from across the country were chosen or signed up to attend the tryouts for the national team. Players put their careers on hold, came home from college and university, and begged bosses for time off to seize the opportunity of a lifetime—an opportunity many never thought they'd live to see. In Manitoba, only three women answered the call for players to attend the provincial camp. In Quebec and New Brunswick, players like France St. Louis and Stacy Wilson got the phone calls every player dreams about, asking them if they'd be interested in playing for Team Canada.

In Ontario, where the number of female hockey players was much higher (largely thanks to the emergence of the COWHL), an open tryout was held to choose 12 players. More than 60 women showed up. The players crammed together on the ice in Mississauga over Thanksgiving weekend in October 1989, with little opportunity to impress among a sea of competitors.

Angela's reputation alone made her a shoe-in to be chosen as one of the 12 Ontarians who made it through for the national tryout, along with COWHL colleagues Cathy Phillips, Geraldine Heaney, Sue Scherer and Margot Verlaan. "I can remember distinctly trying out and thinking, 'Wow, how great is this?'" says Cathy. "I should be at work right now, but I am playing hockey. This is fantastic."

Nevertheless, the path to representing Canada would not be so smooth for Cathy or for Angela. Making it out of Ontario was just half the battle. Now the stakes were higher and the talent pool deeper. Reputation alone wouldn't guarantee a spot on the Canadian roster. Cathy was beginning to really feel the effects of her soon-to-be-discovered brain tumour. Yet she knew this would be her only chance to compete internationally and was not going to let on that she wasn't at 100 percent.

In January 1990, 46 players from across Canada congregated at Meadowvale Four Rinks Complex in Mississauga, ready to battle for the 20 spots available. Players would have to re-learn how to body-check, but this wouldn't be a problem for Angela—although her aggressive play may have hurt her status during the tryout. "I remember that training camp really well: high tempo, lots of hitting, lots of scoring," she says. "They told me to stop hitting as I was hitting too hard. But I was getting hit. So I didn't think that was really fair."

After a mix of practices and intersquad games, 14 players were chosen and announced to great fanfare, with a media conference at the famous Hot Stove Lounge in Maple Leaf Gardens. The CAHA wanted to make a splash and attempted to create a sense of excitement, hosting the announcement at the centre of the hockey universe in Toronto. However, the media coverage was disappointingly weak. General interest in the woman's game was still very low.

Having her name announced at Maple Leaf Gardens as a member of Team Canada would have been a proud, exciting moment for Angela, but instead, it was a big letdown. It turned out Angela's hard hitting style during camp did end up hurting her, as her name was not on the list. She was told she was one of the players, along with Quebec's star France St. Louis, still "being looked at."[2] Her exclusion sent shock waves through the team. "I know the tone in the dressing room from that first group of players was, 'Why am I here if Angela isn't?'" says Fran Rider. "That's how much the players felt for her."

"Well they knocked on your door early in the morning, and basically told you if you made the team or if you didn't," says Angela. "They said to me, 'You weren't selected, but you weren't released either. We just don't know what we're doing basically.' I was really upset. But I knew that there was still room for people to play. It was out of my control."

Uncertain of her future with Team Canada, Angela went home to continue her season with Mississauga. The one extra "look" that was apparently needed to determine her fate never happened. In the wake of this snub, Angela took to the ice with a bur under her saddle, figuring that the CAHA brain trust would be in the stands, but they did not come to watch her play. She received a phone call less than a week later telling her she was in. "What changed?" wonders Angela. "Maybe they did it to get a reaction?"

It was a good question. Whatever changed for Angela also changed for France St. Louis, who was also invited back. Was it a way of getting a reaction, bringing the most well-known of the team's players down a notch, letting the team know who was in charge? There is no doubt Angela would have spoken her mind when she was told to stop hitting during the camp while still having to take hits from others, and perhaps that upset the coaching staff. When it came to selecting players, Angela wonders if Coach McMaster and his staff simply lacked experience. "I just don't think they had a really good handle on the direction they wanted to go," says Angela. "The player evaluation—I don't know who guided that. Maybe they went and got help from somebody."

Whatever the reason for the initial exclusion, the CAHA would not regret its decision to keep Angela, and, despite the minor setback, she had finally reached the summit of competitive hockey. She was going to Ottawa with the elite players from her country to take her game to the world. Upon her Hockey Hall of Fame induction in 2010, she would cite this tournament as her greatest accomplishment. The first one is always the best.

On the eve of this monumental event for international women's hockey, it was like pulling teeth to get any kind of media attention in Canada. The CAHA was extremely concerned that the whole thing would be a public relations flop. They needed something to grab the country's attention and the controversial answer came from Finland.

Tackla, the Finnish hockey equipment manufacturer, approached the IIHF as a potential sponsor with $250,000 to back their pitch. They presented a design for the Canadian jerseys, pants, socks and warm-up gear, which replaced the traditional red and white of Team Canada with shocking hot pink and blue. The hockey pants were unheard of: white, with pink and blue trim. When he first saw the samples, Murray Costello, president of the CAHA, said, "Absolutely not."[3]

Although innovative, the design was simply too much of a departure from traditional Canadian hockey attire. CAHA vice president and future president of Hockey Canada Bob Nicholson was just as adamant in his rejection of the pink plot. "I don't want any part of this," he said.[4] There was a sense of tradition to be upheld and pink would an embarrassment. Yet Murray and his fellow CAHA executives knew something had to happen to sell the tournament—and fast. Pat Reid, another CAHA vice president, spearheaded the pink campaign, and he wore Murray down. Promotions for the tournament needed a shot of adrenaline, so Murray finally relented. The girls would wear pink. He knew it was a publicity stunt, pure and simple, but his back was against the wall.

Sadly, but not surprisingly, the pink decision brought a world of attention to the tournament. The fact that women would be competing globally for the first time was instantly trumped by the news of what they'd be wearing. Everybody weighed in. The players were less than thrilled. Angela said the gear made the players look like "pink flamingos," but nobody was about to complain. "Well, we just did what we were told," says Angela. "We just wanted to play hockey and play for our country. And if they told us to wear polka dots, we'd wear polka dots."

In Brian McFarlane's sprawling retrospective of women's hockey in Canada, *Proud Past, Bright Future: One Hundred Years of Canadian Women's Hockey,* he quotes the Ottawa Sun's Jane O'Hara, who called the Canadians' pink outfits "the wussiest uniforms you've ever seen. Real women don't wear pink. Pink does not inspire fear. Pink does not spark aggression. When you think about battling it out in the corners, you do not think pink. As a team colour pink stinks."[5]

Although some were put off by the pink, hockey fans loved it. The uniforms led to pink madness across Ottawa: pink drinks, pink pom poms, banners, bow ties—pink everything. As a marketing ploy, pink was a big success. Much to the players' relief, it would be a one shot deal. With the public relations game out of the way, it was time to play hockey. As it turned out, Angela and the rest of Team Canada could have been wearing space suits. Perhaps that would have levelled the competition.

Canada's first game was on March 19, 1990, against Sweden. Their pool also included West Germany, and Japan, while in the other pool were the United States, Norway, Finland, and Switzerland. Angela played on a line with fellow Ontarians Margot Page and Kim Ratushny, who was playing hockey at Cornell University. The tone was set early, thanks to the Ontario line. With her mother and siblings in attendance, Angela scored the first goal of the tournament—the first goal ever for Canada in sanctioned international play—1:29 into the game. The final score was 15–1 for Canada. Angela ended up with four goals on that day, and she was just getting warmed up.

Despite the lopsided Canadian victory, the executives at The Sports Network, Canada's first all-sports cable television station, liked what they saw and decided to televise Canada's games for the rest of the tournament; this was a monumental development for a tournament that only a week earlier was begging for any kind of media. Canadians across the nation would finally see its best women players from the comfort of their living rooms and gain a better appreciation for the quality of the women's game. "The TV coverage showed that women's hockey was a very exciting game," Cathy Phillips told Brian McFarlane in 1990. "Parents could see that their daughters could play hockey at a high level, and it was no disgrace to be a female hockey player."[6]

Two nights later, Canada continued its dominance with a 17–0 win against West Germany. Game three saw them beat Japan 18–0, with Angela scoring three goals and sending a Japanese player to the hospital after a crushing hit that broke her leg. This time, the coaching staff did not say anything about her hitting too much. Canada's perfect record took them to the tournament semi-finals against Finland. This was the team's first real test of the tournament, a seesaw affair that ended up with Canada on top 5–4. The United States had defeated Sweden in the other semi-final game, setting the stage for the first of many epic Canada–U.S. championship games.

How Angela and her teammates would react to this kind of pressure remained to be seen, but after countless provincial and national championships, Angela was no stranger to big games. Her coaches had come to realize that she was part of a rare breed of player that craved the spotlight and revelled in high-pressure situations. For Angela, the ice was her sanctuary; it had always been an escape from the uncertainty she'd dealt with since she was a girl. Succeeding in championship games was easy compared to having to scrounge meals or fend off the neighbourhood bully in Flemingdon Park.

"Angela would play her best hockey in big games," says Ken Dufton. "She was the player who wanted to play in big moments. Sometimes, as a coach, when you look down the bench, and you're playing in a national or world championship, you can tell by the body language that some people are a little afraid about being out there. And there are other players, like an Angela James or a Geraldine Heaney, whose body language basically tells you, 'I want to be on the ice. Please put me on the ice.'"

Part of the desire to compete when the stakes are highest comes from confidence, and undoubtedly Angela was confident in her ability as a player. She had enjoyed success at every level, so why should a world championship be any different? Part of her secret was to not over think the situation: just play and everything would take care of itself. "I wasn't really into preparing mentally. That wasn't my thing," says Angela. "I would grab my sticks, re-tape them all and prepare my equipment. I didn't like to get to the rink really early. I don't like a lot of chit-chat before I go and play. Lace 'em up, go do our business."

When Angela and Team Canada took to the ice to face the United States in the first world championship game, it wasn't business as usual. No one on the team could have ever expected what awaited them: the Ottawa Civic Centre was a fury of pink-clad bedlam and the final was played in front of a sold-out crowd. Tickets were impossible to come by. More than 8,700 people showed up—the largest crowd ever to see a women's hockey game. "It was definitely overwhelming at the time and a lot of fun," says Angela. "Being treated like a hockey player, like a star, playing for your country. I think it was all new for everybody, and we were able to display our talents as hockey players. Nobody had really recognized that."

"It was amazing—a packed arena for a women's hockey game," says Fran Rider. "It was spectacular to see all those people cheering for the players, when, in fact, the tone 10 years earlier was to mock and laugh at girls and women with hockey equipment because they weren't supposed to be playing." There was no laughing now, just cheering—although there wasn't much to cheer about from a Canadian perspective in the early minutes of the game. The United States jumped out to a 2–0 lead. The Canadians kept their composure, and stormed back with five unanswered goals to win the game and the tournament. The highlight of the game was a spectacular goal from Geraldine Heaney, which made The Sport Network's list of top plays of that year. France St. Louis, one of those players "still being looked at" during training camp, had two goals and two assists.

In five games played, Angela was Canada's leading scorer with 11 goals and two assists for 13 points, and she was selected to the tournament all-star team. Her teammate Margot Page told Brian McFarlane that during the tournament Angela was the most threatening player on the ice. "She had the skill but she also had everything else," said Margot. "She had the speed and the physical prowess. You couldn't stop her because of that."[7]

The tournament had been a huge success for Angela and an ever bigger one for women's hockey in Canada. In its wake, the CAHA saw a 75 percent increase in the number of registered female players. Ontario accounted for more than half of that surge, with close to 9,000 girls and women playing on 352 teams. "We're doing this for the little girls who are coming up," Angela said during the tournament.[8]

She was right. Brian McFarlane cites a letter written to him by a 12-year-old Mississauga girl named Samantha Holmes, who lived to play hockey and traveled to Ottawa for the first world championship. She wrote how her "friend" Angela James had "given so much to my hockey dreams" and when she scored that first goal, "the moment could not have been more exciting than if my own time [to play] had arrived."[9] When her time did arrive, Samantha made the most of it: she went on to play for Team Canada, earn a scholarship to the University of New Hampshire and start a women's team in Strathmore, Alberta, which competed in the Western Women's Hockey League.

The tournament also affected older women: Elizabeth Etue and Megan Williams, in their influential book *On the Edge: Women Making Hockey History*, tell of an 83-year-old woman who had played in the early 1900s, insisting her son drive her to Ottawa for the tournament so she could see her lifelong dream of a women's world hockey championship come true.[10] As one of Team Canada's most popular players, Angela tried to take this newfound adoration in stride. She was emerging as a positive role model for women—in the male-dominated world of hockey, this was a rare, noteworthy occurrence.

"You know I had some fans, young girls who would look up to me. I realized that," says Angela. "I tried to, as best as I could, behave myself. But there were others as well, older people. I didn't really think of it much. But you are representing your country, and being as successful as we were, there was some popularity amongst different groups. You tried to be gracious about it, knowing very well that one day that will stop. You have to enjoy it while you can."

CHAPTER 8

The Rising

The fantastic growth of women's hockey throughout the early 1990s in Canada was due in large part to the success of the 1990 world championship and the profile of players like Angela. The first-ever women of Team Canada were lauded as heroes—treatment usually reserved for Olympic athletes—and young female hockey players from across Canada now had role models to emulate.

One such player was 15-year-old Cassie Campbell-Pascall, the future captain of Team Canada and three-time Olympian. Cassie remembers the thrill of meeting Angela and the 1990 team when they were celebrated at the Brampton Canadettes' annual tournament. At the time, Cassie was already a member of the Mississauga Warriors—a young girl testing her game against grown women in the COWHL, like Angela before her. "All the girls came in with their pink tracksuits and their medals," remembers Cassie. "I met Angela then and got her autograph. That was a huge moment for me, at 15, to meet those women, to meet your heroes."

Even with the positive aftermath of the tournament, it was still an uphill battle for women to gain respect and an equal footing within the Canadian hockey establishment. One positive change was women's hockey being incorporated into the Canada Winter Games for the first time in 1991, which provided a nation-wide development program for Canadian females under 17 and led to a 40 percent increase in girls registering to play in 1991–92. All of a sudden, each province had means for supporting girls in communities of all sizes.

However, more girls wanting to play meant that ice time was harder to come by, and it was not as though the boys wanted to share; they had had the run of the arenas up to that point and the last thing they wanted was competition for practice time. "There were still a lot of 'old boys' at that point. I am not sure if [women's hockey] was something they wanted to see take off," says Angela. "But I think with the development of the associations in all the provinces, everything was affected. The girls could play as well. Now they needed coaches, and it was a struggle for ice."

It was also a continual struggle for respect and to convince the casual hockey fan that the women's game was skilful, tough and exciting. The world championship had been a big step, and now the country's best players, like Angela, needed to be front and centre to promote the game, whether that meant wearing pink uniforms, or earning credibility with the media. In some cases, earning that credibility meant catering to those ignorant to the women's game and their abilities. Fran Rider recalls how one Toronto newspaper sent out a reporter to interview Angela. The reporter came onto the ice and told Angela to shoot a puck at her. How hard could a woman shoot anyway? "Angela looked at her and said, 'Just wait a second,'" remembers Fran. "She grabbed a puck and fired it against the boards. It didn't take long for the reporter to get off the ice. It is interesting that the reporter came to the game with one feeling about what she was going to be seeing and certainly left with a new appreciation that women could play hockey."

At 27, Angela was now a global star within the world of women's hockey. People would recognize her and ask for her autograph. She had her own hockey card and was leading the Toronto Aeros to provincial championships in the COWHL. The Aeros of the early 1990s boasted many Team Canada members, including Geraldine Heaney, Nathalie Rivard, Heather Ginzel and Margot Verlaan.

Angela was also becoming one of women hockey's best ambassadors—a role that came naturally for her. She lived to play, had boundless charisma and had the enthusiasm to promote the game and teach it to those who had thought about playing but never had the chance. One of those people was Laurie Ikeda, a long-time friend of Angela's, who she met playing softball in 1982. Laurie, a constable with the Toronto Police, had been a lifelong athlete, but had never given hockey a try. Laurie was 27 when Angela finally convinced her to take to the ice.

"I never thought there was women's hockey, Angela basically got me playing," says Laurie. She was an amazing teacher. She could break [the game] down, every single part. She was always encouraging, very patient, very clear. She always had time for everybody."

Laurie's story mirrors that of so many Canadian women, who loved the game but experienced it only as spectators. She continues to play to this day.

Another pair of aspiring players who Angela inspired was Jean Bryant and her partner Shawn Ranahan. Jean and Shawn, both teachers, fell in love with the game, and, like Laurie, both were taken with Angela's skill, teaching ability and enthusiasm for hockey.

"Angela is very good at making you feel like you are really doing well," says Jean. "And she values you as much as she would a world class hockey player. She was a natural at teaching and running drills and had a really nice way about herself."

The three began talking after practices and games, which eventually led to breakfasts together and a friendship that has grown over the years. Jean and Shawn have a log chalet, just outside in the small village of Saint-Sauveur, Quebec, in the Laurentian Mountains, north of Montreal. This isolated, picturesque location has served as an escape for Angela on many occasions over the years. "Ours is a good place for her to come," says Jean. "We're far enough away that people can't get a hold of her. Her phone rings constantly. I think it's one of the few places where she would come and actually finally relax and sleep in."

With all of Angela's obligations on and off the ice, the chalet allowed her to leave the city and all her responsibilities behind, which wasn't easy for her to do. She was a city girl, and even though she hated the bugs and the wilderness was foreign territory for her, she embraced the serenity it offered. Angela could kick back, laugh, tell stories, and do what she loved best: enjoy her life's game in its purist form. On the frozen pond, Angela, with a grin as big as the Laurentians, would play with the enthusiasm of a 10-year-old. Those, like

Jean, Shawn and Laurie knew that, as tough as Angela was in the heat of competition, she was a big kid at heart, always happy to play and share her love of the game with her friends.

For a sport looking to establish a development system, the participation of its best players is an invaluable asset. This was one of the most important characteristics of women's hockey in Canada: stars like Angela were accessible to those just starting out. Not only were they the faces of the national team, they were the teachers and role models for players of all ages, like Laurie, Jean and Shawn, who would be bitten by the hockey bug. "Hockey is so amazing," says Laurie. "I am so glad I started playing."

As the women's game continued to grow at all levels in Canada, those select few players representing Canada started to receive some of the same treatment given to their male counterparts. Although the old school hockey establishment was still firmly dedicated to breeding and supporting males for the NHL, there was no denying that women's hockey was taking off, and 1992 would bring some game-changing developments.

The second world championship for women's hockey took place in Tampere, Finland. The IIHF decided that the tournament would be played every other year to give nations in Europe and Asia more time to develop players to compete with the North American powerhouses. In preparation for Finland, the Canadian Amateur Hockey Association (renamed the Canadian Hockey Association—CHA), under new Senior Vice President Bob Nicholson, would provide Canada's women the same resources allotted to the men's junior hockey program, including regimented off-ice training and a sports psychologist.

While the psychology aspect wasn't so appealing to Angela, she had already made personal fitness a part of her off-season routine. Although she was active all year round with softball and ball hockey, Angela knew she had to learn to take care of her body and train like the elite athlete she was. "As I got older, I got used to training, and I really enjoyed that," says Angela. "Especially in the 1990s with the national team, we had no choice, really. That's where climb-metrics and speed training came in. I took that part of my sport seriously, but it was really difficult, because it's not like the pros. We had to continue to work and provide for ourselves."

Angela was experiencing the problem faced by countless amateur athletes: even though she was a star in her sport, she had to find a way to pay the bills while continuing to train and prepare for the next competition. It was wonderful to start receiving VIP treatment from Hockey Canada during training camps for world tournaments, but there were still 48 other weeks of the year to think about. Angela never once took for granted the importance of having a good job and maintaining her financial stability; as a child, she had seen how tough life could get when money was tight, and she didn't ever want to go back to that. Throughout Angela's life, all of her success in hockey never amounted to the big payday that NHL stars enjoy. Her partner, Ange, always joked that she was "rich and famous, minus the rich."

With the 1992 World Championship approaching, Angela did her best to balance her career at Seneca College, her COWHL play and preparing for training camp. The approach to choosing the team would differ significantly from the provincial tryouts for the 1990 team. The 1992 squad was handpicked by a new coaching staff: Rick Polutnik, assistant coach from the 1990 team, was promoted to head coach, joined by Pierre Charette from Quebec and a fellow Albertan, the Calgary police constable Shannon Miller. This was Shannon's first time behind Team Canada's bench. Six short years later, she would become the first person to coach a Canadian woman's hockey team at the Olympics.

Along with Angela, there were many players who returned from the 1990 team, including fellow Ontarians Margot Verlaan, Heather Ginzel, Sue Scherer, Geraldine Heaney, Laura Schuler and Dawn

McGuire, as well as France St. Louis and France Montour from Quebec; New Brunswick's Stacy Wilson, and Judy Diduck from Alberta.

Right away, Angela felt the tone of the camp was different. First of all, it would take place overseas in Vierumäki, Finland—an experience in itself, as many of the girls, including Angela, had never been out of Canada. And whether it was the more systematic approach of Team Canada or an increased emphasis on discipline and mental toughness, the girls were put through their paces off the ice in a boot-camp atmosphere as soon as they got off the plane. This didn't sit well with Angela. On the ice, things were fine: Angela was named assistant captain, the team gelled in time for the tournament and they were overflowing with talent. Angela refers to it as the best team she was ever on. In the lead-up to the tournament, however, the isolation and team marches through the Finnish countryside got to her. "I didn't like the whole format of the camp. We were isolated, and I didn't like the way we were doing things," she says. "I liked the ice time and that we could walk to the arena. I wasn't really buying into some of the other stuff, but I understood the team building aspect of it."

The team building focused on how the actions of one person affected the entire group. When some players got into trouble for having guys in their rooms, the whole team had to go running at seven in the morning as a consequence. No fun for anyone, including Angela, who wasn't one for dwelling on the mental side of the game or on power trips. Punishment off the ice would not inspire her to raise her game, and getting mad about it wouldn't help either. Rather than that kind of anger, Angela was driven by the prospect of winning, and Team Canada's prospects for success were quite good when it came time to leave Camp Vierumäki and head to Tampere for the tournament.

The 1992 world championship welcomed new teams Denmark (replacing West Germany) and China (replacing Japan), and body-checking was removed from play. A problem developed for the Chinese team because their coaches and players prepared for the games by studying video footage of the 1990 tournament, when hitting was abundant. They received a string of penalties for illegal hits that put them in an even deeper hole than they had already were as they tried to hold their own with the more experienced North American and European teams.

Representatives from the International Olympic Committee (IOC) were in attendance to evaluate the competition and decide whether women's hockey was a viable Olympic sport, but despite the added attention and the excitement that had been generated from the 1990 championship, the media hardly paid the tournament any mind. It wasn't televised, and from all of Canada, only two reporters covered the games. One of them was Robin Brown, who followed the games for CBC Radio. "I was the only Canadian radio reporter there," remembers Robin. "It's amazing how little attention it got over there. From the local press, there was nothing."

Sadly, most of Canada missed a dominant performance. Team Canada extended its undefeated streak at the World's to 10. They breezed through the round-robin beating China, Denmark and Sweden. In the semi-finals, they defeated Finland 6–2 before demolishing the United States 8–0 in the finals. Angela had two goals in the final game. The bronze medal game was an exciting 5–4 shootout win for host Finland over Sweden—a game that ended up being quite influential in the IOC's evaluation of the tournament and their eventual decision to recommend women's hockey as an Olympic sport. "As much as is written about Canada and the U.S., the game between those two countries [Sweden and Finland] was so powerful," says Fran Rider. "It played a big role in getting women's hockey into the Olympics because the [IOC] report was obviously favourable."

At the tournament, the IOC also saw a fast, exciting and high-scoring Canadian team that took advantage of larger international-sized ice surface and played as a cohesive unit that could not be matched by any other team in the world. At the time, head coach

Rick Polutnik complemented his team's response to his approach, team marches and all. "Their thirst for knowledge is great and their commitment to a team concept makes it easy to coach them in a short term competition," said Rick. "All in all it was a great experience. I have a set of memories I'll treasure forever."[1]

Angela turning up ice for Team Canada.

The 1992 Team Canada World Champions.
No. 8 is at back right.

For Angela it was a memorable tournament for many reasons. She was named to the all-star team, with seven points in five games and a plus/minus of plus-7. She admits that Finland was one of her stronger performances and she was amazed at how well the team came together. "It was 'clickity, clickity, click,'" she says. "Everybody was playing really strongly. It was a nice time, and the Fins did a good job hosting."

Off the ice, Angela took full advantage of the Finnish hospitality. It was her first time in Europe and she wanted to make the most of it. Luckily, she had her own personal tour guide in the form of Sari Krooks, her teammate with the Aeros and member of Team Finland. Angela stayed afterwards and travelled through Sweden and Germany for two weeks with Sari and Geraldine Heaney. The fun started as soon as Sari pulled up in her car, which was as luxurious as Angela's back home. "It was a Lade. It had no heat," says Angela. "I am surprised it even had a floor in the thing. Sari took us into Germany onto the Autobahn, which was disgusting. But we had an awesome trip. It was a lot of fun."

The experiences Angela had playing hockey were fulfilling for her on many levels. She has always said, "Thank God for sports," and this sentiment is echoed by the many things she saw and did as a result of her outstanding athletic skills. In 1993, for example, she returned to Germany to compete for Canada in the world roller hockey championships under head coach Ken Dufton. Along with Geraldine Heaney, Angela led Canada to an unexpected championship—the team having been ranked dead last in the tournament. She also earned the nickname "Maradona" from the European fans, for her charismatic personality and the way she dominated the play, just as Diego Maradona once did on the soccer pitch. "That was an amazing experience," says Ken. "You saw Angela's natural athleticism. It took her virtually no time, I mean she had to get used to her [roller] skates like the rest did, and the stick, but once she did, look out!"

Angela enjoyed whatever she did, never taking herself too seriously. It was always a thrill for her to compete. As a kid, it was her way out of dangerous situations, and as an adult, it was a way to share her talents with her teammates and her country. In 1994, there was another chance to compete globally at the next world championship in Lake Placid, New York. The stakes were even higher for this tournament, and all those that followed, thanks to what took place in late in 1992.

On November 17, 1992, the International Olympic Committee had announced that women's hockey would be part of the 1998 Olympics in Nagano, Japan. The Committee had been more than impressed with the level of competition and the skills possessed by the world's best players in Finland, and saw the potential of women's hockey as an Olympic sport. This was the announcement every player, volunteer and fan wanted to hear. It was the ultimate goal for the sport, and it had been achieved after only two world tournaments.

"Women's hockey in the Olympics will have a major impact on the entire sport throughout the world," Fran Rider told Brian McFarlane at the time. "It will bring out the young players and will open the doors for the kind of government and corporate support that has not been there for non–Olympic sports. Young people can now see the light at the end of the tunnel; something they could never see before."[2]

Fran recalls how women's hockey was almost a part of the 1994 Olympics in Lillehammer, Norway. However, the $1 million price tag was too high to incorporate the event so close to the Games, and the Norwegians declined to add it. This was a decision that would haunt many of the veterans of Team Canada, including Angela. "It was a disappointment because, again, the reason we're in the Olympics is the quality of the players that got us there," says Fran. "Players in all countries lost the opportunity to play because of the four year wait."

At the time, no one was thinking of a missed opportunity in Lille-hammer, there was only elation. Women's hockey had reached the pinnacle. Every game and every tournament from that moment on would be played with only one thing in mind: preparing for the Olympics. The timing could not have been better for Angela, as she was at the height of her game, and there were two more world championships that would give her the chance to refine her skills and grow accustomed to the Team Canada system. For the 1993–94 COWHL season, she left the powerhouse Aeros to play for the upstart Scarborough Red Wings. She was drawn to the challenge of helping a less-talented team. While the Wings could not knock off the Aeros in league play, Angela benefited from the experience of leading a less experienced group of players,. As the 1994 World Championships in Lake Placid approached, she was ready and she knew the stakes were higher than ever.

The 1994 Team Canada line-up was an indicator that the core talent pool for Canadian women's hockey was changing. Only six members of the 1990 and 1992 teams remained, including Angela, the ageless France St. Louis, Geraldine Heaney, Judy Diduck, Margot Page and Stacy Wilson. Younger players like defenceman Cheryl Pounder and goaltender Lesley Reddon were now challenging for positions previously held by veterans on the roster, and looking to show the world what they could do for Team Canada.

Two of the most noteworthy additions to the team were defence-man Cassie Campbell-Pascall and 15-year-old Hayley Wickenheiser. Hayley was making her debut on the world stage en route to becoming the face of women's hockey for the next 17 years. Cassie had been cut from the 1990 and 1992 teams, and now, at age 20, surprised everyone with an outstanding camp, securing a spot on the squad she would eventually lead as captain. Cassie is a student of the game and respectful of its rich history; being around team veterans like Angela offered her an even greater perspective of the amazing heights they were reaching together.

"It gave me a sense of tradition about our game," says Cassie. "To remember women like Angela and France St. Louis and what they had to go through to give my generation this moment."

Hayley, the teenage phenom of the 1994 team, was in awe of her surroundings, as any young person would be. She was thrown directly into the fire. Head Coach Les Lawton from Concordia University stuck her on the top line, alongside Angela and Stacy Wilson. It didn't take long for Hayley to see what made Angela a special player, and she would emulate her physical style in her own game. "Angela was very intense, driven, with a desire to win," says Hayley. "On the ice, she was a fierce competitor. You know, she could be very demanding of herself and of the players around her. She just wanted to be the best."

Indeed, the respect was mutual. Angela saw right away the special talent Hayley possessed and knew what a benefit she would be to the team, even at such a young age. Angela welcomed her with the good natured ribbing reserved for all young players, giving her the nicknames "Rookie" and "High Hair Hayley" for her impressive blonde do.

After a surprising exhibition game loss to Finland, the Canadians got down to business maintaining a 3–0 record during round robin play and defeating Finland 4–1 in the semi finals. The United States, having defeated the Chinese team in their semi-final game, would once again face Canada in the finals.

Coach Lawton, along with his assistants Melody Davidson and Shannon Miller, were aware the United States would be feeding off the home crowd and the ghosts of the 1980 "Miracle on Ice," when the United States Men's Olympic Team had upset the heavily-favoured Soviet Red Army on that same ice surface. But Angela wasn't afraid of ghosts.

The final game saw Angela at her most dominant, game-changing best. After Team Canada fell behind 1–0 in the first period, Danielle

Goyette scored to tie it early in the second. That's when Angela put the team on her back, leading the charge with two almost identical goals—both end-to-end rushes, less than three minutes apart. The second goal was started by her linemate Hayley Wickenheiser, who had returned to action after being sidelined by an injury. "I remember having the feeling of 'I've got to get the puck to her,'" remembers Hayley. "I chipped the puck off the boards, she took it and drove their defenceman wide and went in and scored."

Angela's second goal was worthy of a highlight reel, showcasing her speed, finesse and strength on the puck. What was most impressive was that she blew past Kelly O'Leary, one of the best U.S. defencemen, on the play, faking a slap shot, then beating her wide to the net and scoring with a backhand.

"Angela made [O'Leary] look silly," remembers Cassie. "We were down in the game and she took it over. It was probably one of the best individual performances I have seen in my career. She turned it up to another gear. Nobody could touch her. It was the 'AJ show' in 1994."

In the Sports Network's footage of Angela during the final game, what stands out the most is her vision on the ice. She possessed the rare ability to anticipate where the puck was going and how to find her teammates with crisp passes, providing them with good scoring opportunities. While so much is made of Angela's shot and her skating ability, it is forgotten that she was also an outstanding playmaker who did the "little" things necessary to win.

As a centre, one of her biggest responsibilities was to win faceoffs. This was something she could do almost at will, giving her team possession of the puck at the beginning of each play—an important advantage that can swing the momentum of a game very quickly.

Indeed, Angela's size and strength were assets too, and she used them to her full advantage. She was very good at using her body to shield the puck from opposing players, keeping them to the outside while she would drive towards the net using her powerful legs.

Footage of Angela also reveals what a strong skater she was. Her long strides and hunched-over skating style—another trait she shared with Wayne Gretzky—kept her centre of gravity low, making it extremely difficult for opponents to out-muscle her or take the puck away.

Angela's two goals had put Canada up 3–1, but as the second period of the 1994 final game wore on, the Americans gained some momentum. A penalty to Geraldine Heaney led to a power play goal, and the chants of "U.S.A., U.S.A." bellowed through the arena. Geraldine took another penalty minutes later, but thanks to some great penalty killing by Angela and her teammates, the score remained 3–2 as period two came to a close.

The Canadians came out for the third period with their guns blazing. The United States took an early penalty, and Danielle Goyette capitalized with a power play goal (her second of the game) to make the score 4–2. Both teams played desperate, physical hockey, fighting for every loose puck, hacking each other with their sticks and chirping at each other after every whistle. The heated rivalry they shared was clear.

Stacy Wilson scored Canada's fifth goal, increasing their lead to three. This would be huge for the Canadians, as the Americans would answer less than a minute later thanks to future Hall-of-Famer Cammi Granato.

With the score 5–3 for Canada, the next goal would provide the scoring team with a massive shift in momentum. Canada could smell that victory was near, and was not going to give the U.S. a chance to scratch their way back. Along with Angela, another veteran presence on Team Canada was the captain, France St. Louis. France caught the U.S. deep in the Canadian's zone and led a three-on-one break, which resulted in a beautiful goal that sealed the Canadians' victory. The score was 6–3, and Canada had a third straight World Championship, won right in the back yard of their hated rivals. The announced crowd for the final was 3,198 and more than half were Canadians.[3]

Angela was on the ice for the final seconds of the game, and when the final horn sounded, she mobbed her teammates, all smiles with three fingers in the air, marking the Canadian "three-peat." Sue Scherer, colour commentator for The Sports Network, and Angela's former teammate, commented during the telecast, that Angela "has been a great player for a long time" and had a "bright future ahead of her."

Angela was named MVP of the final game, but, as always, diverted the recognition to her team and the importance of the win. "There's only one MVP, but there are 20 gold medals, and that's what's important," she said at the time. "Our edge is our coaching staff."[4] What followed was a big party in Lake Placid and an even bigger storm, which kept everyone snowed in for a day after the finals. Nobody seemed to mind, as many players had friends and family in attendance to share in the spectacular accomplishment, including Angela. She would call it the best individual performance of her career at any level. She had nine points in five games, but what was more impressive was her ability to raise her game when the stakes were highest. She was a "big game player" who, at age 29, was making a strong case for being the best player in the world.

As Team Canada teammate Margot Page told Scott Russell in 2000, "She was the most threatening player on the ice. She had the skill, but she also had the speed and the physical prowess. You couldn't stop her because of that. It wasn't just her skill level that set her apart. It was her competitive nature that made her great."[5]

In Lake Placid, that greatness was in full bloom for all to see. Nagano was less than four years away. The Olympics would be the culmination of all Angela had strived for as a player—every bus ride to the rink, every practice, every battle she had won on and off the ice had led to this. It was her dream, and it was right before her eyes for the taking.

CHAPTER 9

Changing of the Guard

After the 1994 victory in Lake Placid, Angela's life off the ice took an unexpected turn for the better. When she was least expecting it, she met her life partner, by chance, in a downtown Toronto bar. Not surprisingly, there was a hockey connection.

Angela "Ange" McDonald, a former police officer, had come to Toronto from her home of Prince Edward Island in 1988. She was from a big family (five brothers and a sister) who lived in Kellys Cross, Queens County—midway across the island, very close to the south shore. An A-level hockey player in Eastern Canada, Ange left home to pursue her police training and ended up working for the 52 Division of the Toronto Police Force until 1993. Police work took its toll; although she met many dedicated, passionate officers, she also saw a great deal of cynicism and corruption. Ange worked undercover attempting to combat prostitution in downtown Toronto, but when a move to a less stressful assignment didn't come, she left the force.

On that fateful night in May 1994, romance was the last thing on 29-year-old Ange's mind; she had just come out of a long-term relationship and was recovering from a bad car accident. It was a friend's birthday and she was looking for nothing more than a night out and a good time. Then Angela James asked her to dance.

"We were dancing," remembers Ange. "And it was quite dark. We got to talking and believe it or not, by the end of the night, we were talking hockey. I was looking to play with a team, I said, 'Do you play hockey?' And Angela said, 'I play a little bit.'" The joke was Ange had grown up idolizing Angela James, the hockey player. But when they first met in person, she did not recognize her in the dark, smoky bar. By the end of the night, Ange clued in that her dance partner was her hockey hero and figured there was no chance for anything serious— dating the hockey star she knew from TV would be just too weird. Yet at the same time, she was taken with how nice and down-to-earth Angela was. Ange even tried to set Angela up with her friend, but Angela wasn't having any of that. She told Ange where she worked and asked her to call. The problem was, when Ange tried to call Angela at Seneca, she called the wrong college—Centennial. (It must have been really loud in the bar that night.) When there was no Angela James to be found, she figured she'd been fed a line. Luckily, their paths crossed again three weeks later and the college-confusion was cleared up. Some lengthy phone calls followed, and before Ange knew it, she'd been invited to a birthday party for Angela's mom—a big step to say the least. Even then, she brought her friend, and again, Angela's attention didn't waiver. "I picked the right one, that's for sure," says Angela.

"At that point, the more time I spent with her, the more I started to really like this person," says Ange. "I didn't care who she was. I idolized her as a child, so be it." From that point, things moved quickly. Less than two years later, Ange had moved into the house Angela was renting with three others in Toronto. Three months later, the two went their own way and started renting in a triplex at the north end of the city. In May 1996, Angela and Ange gathered family and friends at the United Church in Richmond Hill, just north of Toronto, for a commitment ceremony to announce their love to the world and celebrate their lifelong devotion. This was five years before same-sex marriage was legalized in Canada. The ceremony marked an important milestone for Angela: her relationship with Ange brought her the stability she had not experienced as a child and the chance to start a family of her own. Her folks were thrilled, and although Ange and Donna tended to butt heads, she accepted Ange into the family. Yet the idea of two women acknowledging their love for each other publically was not easy for everyone to accept, including Angela's sister Kym.

"Kym didn't bring my niece or nephew to the ceremony," says Angela. "She thought they shouldn't be exposed to that. Now, I think in hindsight, she probably kicks herself for being that way. But that was her view, so we had to respect it at that time." Kym's hesitancy would fade as she saw the great team the two Angela's made. They share some intangible traits: loyalty, devotion to family, the importance of humour and having fun with whatever you do. Yet in some ways they are opposites too: where Ange is serious-minded, Angela is more laid back—that is until she gets on the ice. In the coming years, Angela would face the most serious challenges of her career, and Ange would be by her side every step of the way.

The happy couple in the early days of their relationship.

From 1995 through 1997, the opportunities for international competition expanded in the lead up to the first Olympic Games that would feature women's hockey. In 1995, San Jose California hosted the first ever Pacific Rim Championship (now called the Pacific Women's Hockey Championship), which included only four teams:

Canada, the United States, China and Japan. This small tournament was seen as an opportunity to provide some of Team Canada's younger players with more international experience. The recently-promoted head coach of the Canadian program was Shannon Miller. At 31, Shannon was considered a wunderkind by the Team Canada executives, who would allow her to run the program for the next three years. Described by Toronto Star sports writer Damien Cox as "an intriguing character with the eye of a tiger and the deft touch of a diplomat,"[1] Shannon stressed control and discipline in her coaching philosophy and had "become a key role model for players and coaches,"[2] including young Hayley Wickenheiser.

Shannon had her eyes firmly set on the future. The youth of the Canadian program was her number one priority, and the team's veterans were put on notice. "You may have some old, experienced veterans, but they still only know what's best for them," she told Cox in an interview. "The coach knows what's best for the whole team."[3]

This quote is a telling insight about Shannon's outlook and desired team make-up. She would not have been much older than many of the Team Canada veterans—younger than some—and perhaps saw them as a threat to her authority and ability to win the hearts and minds of the younger players on her team. As it turned out, Shannon chose only seven members of the 1994 world championship team to mentor the next generation of national stars during the Pacific Rim tournament. Angela James was not one of them.

No one thought anything of this exclusion, including Angela. Nor should they have. She was coming off the strongest international performance of her career in Lake Placid and was one of the cornerstones of Team Canada's women's program. She was glad to have some stability in the Team Canada coaching staff, having seen Shannon work her way up from an assistant coach in 1992 to the big job in 1995. "It's really nice to have Shannon, who has been there for a number of years," Angela said at the time. "I think you need that. Shannon has some insights and has seen different things. When you are in constant change with coaching staff it makes it difficult."[4]

The following year, Angela did participate in the Pacific Rim tournament, leading Canada to another victory with seven points in five games. Later that year, in October 1996, Shannon named Angela the captain of Team Canada's entry in the first ever Three Nations Cup, held in Ottawa, Ontario, with games also taking place in Kingston, Ontario, and Canton, New York. This tournament included the world's top three hockey nations: Canada, the U.S. and Finland. Canada suffered its second-ever defeat in international play, a 2–1 overtime loss to the U.S. This defeat was quickly erased with a 1–0 win over them in the finals on the same Ottawa Civic Centre ice that hosted the first world championships six years earlier. That win solidified Shannon's bid for the job of head coach of Canada's Olympic team.

For Angela, this tournament was not a good one: her point production was nowhere near what it had been, she only had two assists in five games and, during the loss to the Americans, she wasn't put on the ice during the overtime period. This benching confused Angela. There was no explanation from Shannon or any indication that there was something in Angela's game that was lacking, defensively or otherwise. Angela was frustrated by the silent treatment; it didn't help to improve her play or the relationship between player and coach.

"If you've got a team and you've got good players working towards something, you want to work with a player to improve the situation," says Angela. "You take them aside and have them work on it or have an [assistant] coach work on those areas. That's how it would be if I were coaching."

Adding to the bad taste of the Three Nations Cup was an incident that took place off the ice. From as early as her childhood in Flemingdon Park, Angela has been subject to racial slurs, which would continue now and again as she grew up, sometimes on the ice.

As a kid, she'd respond with her fists, but on the ice, it was with a thunderous hit—like the one she delivered during a national championship one year when a French-Canadian player taunted her with calls of "blackie, blackie." The culprit left the ice on a stretcher.

What happened to Angela during the Three Nations Cup blindsided her in many ways. Here she was, one of the stars of her game, a 31-year-old adult representing her country in the nation's capital; the colour of her skin, or anyone else's, was the furthest thing from her mind.

"As you get older and become an adult, you don't really expect that kind of thing," says Angela. "At the Three Nations Cup, there were some guys in the hotel, partying. One said 'Hey everyone, come on in, yeah, except for that nigger out there. Stay out there.' I had to deal with that. I had to go back to bed and try to get ready to play in this championship, and I couldn't believe that I had just experienced something like that. Here you are representing your country, and somebody is saying that to you."

In retrospect, Angela tries to downplay that incident by qualifying it as "minor" and pointing out that the racism she's experienced as a hockey player doesn't compare to what many other athletes had to endure. Yet the clarity with which she recalls what happened that night in Ottawa shows that those words stayed with her. How could they not? Over the years, Angela's skin had thickened to this kind of ignorance, but on this night she was the captain of Team Canada, staring at the ceiling of her hotel room with the sting of racism in her ears. It seemed as though things were going from bad to worse.

Angela could also see that her role on the national team was starting to change. She wasn't the go-to offensive option anymore. Younger players like Hayley Wickenheiser, Jayna Hefford and Nancy Drolet were coming to the forefront, eating up more time on the power play and penalty killing units. Despite this shift, Angela's focus remained the same: prepare for the Olympics. The 1997 world championships would be the final international event before Nagano. It would also serve as the Olympic qualifying tournament to determine which six countries would earn the right to compete in the Games.

For the first time since 1990, the world championship would be played in Canada. The host city was Kitchener, Ontario, with games also being held across province in Brampton, Bradford, Hamilton, London, Mississauga and North York. Canada did not disappoint the hometown fans, including the 6,247 people who packed the Kitchener Auditorium for the tournament's final game (the largest hockey crowd in the building's history). The Sports Network reported 400,000 viewers per minute during the final, with a peak of 700,000 during the last half hour.

The capacity crowd in Kitchener and viewers across Canada were treated to a classic Canada-U.S. battle, which Canada won 4–3 in overtime. Nancy Drolet got the winner—her third of the game. Angela also had a goal in the final, her second of the tournament and fifth point in five games—lower totals than her previous world competitions. Though Coach Miller had depended on her at crucial moments throughout the tournament,[5] she was, again, left on the bench during the overtime period. The writing was on the wall: Angela's value in the eyes of the Team Canada coaching staff was lessening. Still, as one of the best players in the world and a veteran of seven years of international play, she could see that her contribution to Team Canada going forward would be different. It was a strange feeling for the lifelong superstar, but she was fine with it. Regardless of her job on the team, be it on the first line or the fourth, Angela's ultimate goal had not changed: she'd carry the puck bag, so long as she was on the flight to Nagano. Both her experience and her reputation for rising to the occasion during the biggest games would be invaluable in the Olympic pressure cooker.

"I have been pretty fortunate because I have had to deal with the international scene for a number of years now," Angela said in 1998. "So for me it is pretty easy. I know what to expect because I have gone through it. So it isn't a surprise. I am not a real excitable person as it is. I try not to let my emotions get the best of me."[6]

After taking some time off in the summer to rest up and prepare herself for the biggest challenge of her life, Angela headed to Calgary for training camp. She was greeted with the news that she'd be playing on the fourth line and taken off the power play and penalty killing units. She had a sick feeling in her stomach and she didn't feel at all herself. Things would only get worse. "It was a month into camp, and I knew something had gone wrong," Angela told Scott Russell in 2000. "I knew they wanted to release me."[7]

CHAPTER 10

Shattered Dream

For three straight days in the first week of December 1997, Angela lay in her Calgary apartment, crying. Family, friends, co-workers, former coaches and teammates kept calling, but she was too distraught to speak to anyone. The 32-year-old was still struggling to cope with the realization that her dream was over.

Seventy-two hours earlier, Shannon Miller had instructed Angela to come to her office for a 10 a.m. meeting. No one else at the Olympic training camp was asked to attend this meeting, which immediately raised Angela's suspicions. Waiting in the office along with Shannon were her two assistant coaches, Ray Bennett and Daniele Sauvageau. When Angela sat down, Shannon wasted little time. Shaking her head, she looked the star forward dead in the eyes and said, "Sorry, you didn't make it. Your best wasn't good enough." Angela's heart sank to the bottom of her stomach. Utter silence soon fell over the room. Devastated, Angela stood up and told her coaches "A dog would have been treated better," before storming out of the office. In utter shock, Angela didn't speak to any of her teammates. She threw on her Team Canada jacket, walked out of the Olympic Oval training facility and headed straight to her car. She started the engine and drove off.

On December 9, Hockey Canada held an official press conference to announce the players that would make up Canada's first women's Olympic hockey team. After the 20 names were read, every reporter in the room had their hands up, waiting to ask the head coach the same question: "Why did you cut Angela James?" Shannon, who was on sabbatical from the Calgary police force to coach the women's team, defended her stunning decision. "The game has changed," she said. "It's a lot faster. More team play is necessary. Angela has been very strong for us in the individual type of play. She was struggling with the execution of team play. At the same time, we had different players who could produce offensively. I don't think she was totally surprised."[1]

Before the press conference was over, Shannon fired some more parting shots Angela's way, including calling her a "defensive liability" and reinforcing to those in the audience, who were still scratching their collective heads, that the team's selections were based on "talent and character."[2]

The very next day, news of Angela's release made national headlines in Canada. Angela was enraged when she learned of Shannon's comments. Before packing her bags to head back to Toronto, Angela spoke with reporter Joe Warmington to share her side of the story. During the interview, she told Warmington that she felt "set-up and cheated."[3] "They did everything in their power to keep me down. I don't know what their agenda was," she said. "Maybe they thought I was an old hag and shouldn't be around or maybe it was because I received too much attention."[4]

The most telling piece of information Angela shared with Warmington was a conversation she had with Shannon two weeks before the team was announced. Angela said that at the time, Shannon told her "she was playing well and had nothing to fear."[5] As it turned out, that couldn't have been further from the truth.

On the long drive home to Toronto, replaying everything that had happened, Angela kept coming back to the same question: why? In 13 preliminary games, she had seven goals—the most on the team—and four assists. Most importantly, all of Angela's points came during five-on-five play, as Shannon rarely used her on the power play.[6] Moreover, leading up to the Olympics, Angela was the most decorated women's player on the planet, with four world championships, and she was Canada's all-time leader in points. On merit alone, many argued, the former team captain should have been named to the team. But like one of her heroes growing up, Mark Messier, who was left off the 1998 men's Olympic team, Angela found herself on the outside looking in. And she wanted answers. She knew she wasn't going to get them in Calgary, or from Shannon, so when Angela arrived in Toronto, she contacted Hockey Canada and demanded a review of her release from the team.

On December 16, Angela met in Kitchener, Ontario, with Canadian Hockey Association president Murray Costello and senior vice president of hockey operations Bob Nicholson to get the answers she was looking for.[7] During their two-hour session, Angela told the hockey executives that she felt her release came without merit and didn't reflect her abilities as a player.[8] Angela said she had one conversation with Shannon, where she was told she was in the "grey zone." In fact, the entire exchange was recorded for the documentary The Game of Her Life, which chronicled the women's Olympic hockey team from their training camp in Calgary to the Nagano Olympics. As the cameras were rolling, Shannon sat Angela down in her office and said:

> "I still consider you a player that is in the grey area. I do agree you are getting stronger every day, but so is everybody else."

> "Does that encompass everything?" Angela replied, looking for clarification from her coach. "Is this compared to everybody else or is this grey zone area?"

> "Hayley Wickenheiser is going to be on this team," said Shannon. "So there are players like that for us that are there. There are players for us right now that we are not too sure about if they really can step up and play. For example, will some of these rookies that are in the grey area with the veterans, will they replace them? Because we are going to take the best team. You are one of the players that are in the grey area."[9]

During that meeting, or any other time for that matter, Angela cannot remember Shannon or any of the other coaches telling her that she wasn't a "team player" or a "defensive liability." "I understand at some point your hockey goes down, but at 32 I was feeling pretty strong," says Angela. "I was still producing and playing well. If I was seen as a defensive liability, say something, work with me, keep the line of communications open to fix it. Nobody said anything."

After her meeting with Murray and Bob, Angela wasn't sure how the ruling would go, but felt optimistic. What happened next would once again shock the hockey world.

Two days after meeting with Angela, Murray and Bob were set to meet with the national team coaching staff when a media fire storm erupted after accusations surfaced of an alleged romantic relationship between Shannon and women's team captain Stacy Wilson.[10] The rumour was just that, a rumour, but it didn't take long for people to accuse Angela of making the allegations, given the timing of the review into her release. "Here I am trying to get some answers and meanwhile I have all the media calling me a suck," recalls Angela. "I told them [these rumours] have nothing to do with me."

Murray met with Shannon and her assistants, and he believed the head coach when she assured him she wasn't having an affair with her captain. In his investigation, Murray determined the rumour came from a third party that was trying to create controversy on the team.[11] On the issue of Angela's release, to almost no one's surprise, Murray and Bob sided with the coaching staff they had handpicked. "After talking to the coaches, I believe the decision was well thought out, and the player evaluations were detailed and documented," said Murray at the time.[12] "All the games were documented and the players rated after each game."[13]

With that decision, Angela's Olympic dream was officially over. Meanwhile, Shannon felt vindicated and was certain she had selected the team that would win the first gold medal in women's ice hockey. "The best team has been chosen and the best team is going," she said. "Unless somebody tells me otherwise, Angela James is not on its roster."[14]

Indeed, the Canadian women's hockey team went to the 1998 Nagano Winter Olympics without Angela. As expected, the team made it to the gold medal game. Waiting for them was the United States, led by Captain Cammi Granato. Coming into the Olympics, Canada had dominated the Americans in international play, and despite losing 7–4 to them early in the tournament, the Canadians were still favoured to win. Before a global audience, in what is still considered to be the most significant game in the history of women's hockey, the Canadians came up short.

For all the talk of Shannon Miller's coaching prowess, her team came out flat and looked scared as they took the ice at the Big Hat Arena in central Nagano. Right from the puck drop, Canada was clearly on the defensive, trying its best to stave off a relentless U.S. attack. The first period ended scoreless thanks to the strong play of Canadian netminder Manon Rheaume. The second period, however, saw the U.S. continue to pour on the pressure, and at 2:38 on the power play they struck first blood on a goal from Gretchen Ulion. Midway through the third period, the U.S. scored a second power play goal by Shelley Looney. With time running out, Canada finally woke up at the 15:59 mark when Danielle Goyette managed to beat U.S. goaltender Sarah Tueting. But it was too little too late. With a minute left to go and with the Canadian goalie pulled, the U.S. scored on the empty net. The game had ended. The American players tossed their sticks and gloves up in the air, and piled on top of each other at centre ice in celebration. The final score was 3–1 and the U.S. had captured the historic first Olympic gold medal in women's ice hockey.

Back home in Toronto, Angela's family was celebrating. Cindy and Kym watched the game together, and every time the U.S. scored they jumped up off the sofa and screamed. For the sisters, and their entire family, Canada's loss was vindication for Angela's dismissal from a hockey program she had helped build. "I was never so hurt and disappointed for my sister," says Cindy. "After everything she's given and done for women's hockey to have not played in the Olympics. It broke our hearts."

Unlike her family, Angela chose not to watch the gold medal game. She was back to work at Seneca and was trying desperately to move on after the Olympic fiasco. When she found out Team Canada had lost, her thoughts immediately turned to her former teammates, some of whom she had gone to battle with for close to two decades. "My heart went out to every single player on that team," says Angela.

In the years ahead, the Canadian women's team would strike gold many times, but this historic first loss hung over the heads of many of Angela's teammates, who were still upset about her exclusion. At the time, some of them, like Cassie Campbell-Pascall, were young and hesitant to speak up. But, to this day, the former Canadian women's captain and two-time gold medal winner can't understand why her friend and teammate was left off the 1998 team. "I think a lot of people looked at our coach and thought, 'What the heck are you thinking?'" says Cassie. "I think it made us question our coach, that decision."

Despite not being the number one or two centre at the time, Cassie felt Angela could have easily been slotted on the wing on any of the top lines. Instead, during the camp Shannon relegated her to the fourth line, where she saw her ice time quickly diminish. "Angela would be the first person to tell you that she didn't have the greatest Olympic training camp that year," says Cassie. But there was good reason. Angela was suffering from an undiagnosed thyroid condition that was sapping her energy and dropped her down to 150 pounds—20 pounds under her regular playing weight. Even though Angela told the coaches she wasn't feeling well, none of Team Canada's medical staff could figure out what was ailing her. "It's not a matter if someone's tired or not feeling well," an unsympathetic Shannon said to Angela during camp. "But it's the attitude of 'I am not scared to fail, and I know where I stand and when I look back, no matter what happens, I want to know I gave it absolutely everything I had. There are excuses. I laid myself on the line to make this team.' I don't feel that we are getting that from you."[15]

Although she wasn't 100 percent, Angela gave it her best shot and managed to lead the team in goals during exhibition play. She was producing, which makes Cassie believe the decision to cut Angela was personal. "She should have been put on the wing. She should have had my spot if that was the case. She was a game breaker and someone that you needed on your team. To me, it had to have been personal, that's the only thing I can think of. That was the worst decision ever made. I say it to this day, as loud as I can."

Hayley Wickenheiser, who today is considered to be the greatest woman to ever play the game, was taken aback by the decision to cut Angela. Hayley had rightfully moved into her former linemate's number one spot at centre, but it never crossed her mind that Angela wasn't going to make the team. "I was surprised," she says. "I remember that she came in as a top player that was expected to make it, and had the talent to make it."

Hayley doesn't remember witnessing any problems between Angela and Shannon during the camp. The only tension she could recall came after the fact, when Angela was cut and a war of words followed between the coach and her former player. If Angela had not been cut, Hayley said there definitely would have been a different team dynamic, but she's not sure if the outcome would have changed. "Who knows?" she says. "It could have been. Had we done a lot of things that year, the outcome could have been different."

Ironically, the one person that could truly empathize with what Angela went through in 1998 was fellow 2010 Hockey Hall of Fame inductee Cammi Granato. Prior to the 2006 Olympics, head coach Ben Smith cut the U.S. captain, leaving an entire nation—and its best player—in shock. Her best days might have been behind her, but Cammi still felt she had a lot to give and, like Angela, felt completely blindsided.

"I had no idea it was coming," says Cammi. "I felt so ready to contribute to the Olympics. I had all this energy, so finely tuned. I felt like I was at the top of my game and then to have someone say, 'No, I'm sorry.' It's not like I had an injury. It was very hard to deal with and still is."

Cammi, who calls Angela the most "intimidating, dominant and fierce" player she has ever played against, said she was in disbelief when she learned the Canadian superstar had been released by Team Canada. "How do you take your best player off the team? Your most clutch player off the team? It was really shocking. She brought a lot to Canada in big games."

CBC broadcaster Robin Brown was also critical of Shannon's decision and pulls no punches, describing the move to cut Angela as "appalling." "That whole thing kind of makes me feel ill," says Robin. "I felt very strongly that she should have been on that team on merit and for what she's done for the game. If she wasn't as good as she was a couple of years earlier, you can live with that. Give her a different role on the team. But you don't cut her."

For Murray Costello and Bob Nicholson, Angela's release from the team was more a disappointment than a shock. Bob concedes Angela was still a good player, but she wasn't the prominent player she was back through the 1980s and early 1990s. Both hockey executives said the selection process for the women's team, like the world juniors, is left to the coaching staff. "That's the way it was set out then, "Bob says. "And the process still works the same way today."

To this day, Shannon's assistant coach, Ray Bennett, does not second guess the decision to cut Angela. Ray, then the lone male coach on the staff, says he was "complicit" in all the decisions made by the Team Canada coaching staff, whether that involved player personnel or tactical play. He described Angela as a good teammate who was well liked, but still believes, even today, that she had a bit of a "star" mentality and he wasn't sure she was buying into the team concept, especially defensively. Ray says she worked hard at the game, but was not always a great practice player. Instead, games were her showcase.

"Obviously [Angela] wanted to go to those Olympics," says Ray. "But it didn't work out for her, and as much of a role I played in that, so did she." Ray maintains the coaching staff was thorough in their player selections. The team's goal right from the first day of camp was to win gold, and he still feels the players they took to Nagano gave Canada the best shot to do so. "The task of selecting the team, in my mind, is to select the players who give your team the best chance of winning," he says. "If it is anything else, then as a coaching staff, you are doing a disservice to the team and their goal. Because we did not win gold, we are all open to second guessing and what ifs. But I don't live my life that way."

After the Olympics, Murray and Bob decided not to run a full-time national women's hockey program during the 1998–99 season. As a result, the contracts of head coach Shannon and assistants Daniele and Ray were not renewed. It was announced that Shannon would remain a key part of the national program in an undetermined role. Shannon, however, opted to leave Team Canada. She took her coaching talents south to the United States—the country that she failed to beat when it mattered the most. Today, she is the head coach of the University of Minnesota-Duluth women's hockey program.

Daniele Sauvageau would eventually go on to do what Shannon did not: in 2002, she led the Canadian women's hockey team to its first-ever gold medal in Olympic competition. Ray joined the St. Louis Blues as an assistant in 2006 and has been with the club ever since.

The decision to leave Angela off the 1998 team left a big hole in her heart. It also left her questioning her ability. At 33, she was contemplating quitting the game she had loved since she was six years old.

CHAPTER 11

Calling it a Career

After a short, self-imposed hiatus, Angela was back on the ice playing with her club team the Toronto Aeros, having rejoined them after a stint with the Scarborough Red Wings. Head Coach Ken Dufton was thrilled to have his prized player back, but took one look at her and knew something was terribly wrong. For starters, Angela was at least 20 pounds lighter. She lacked speed and energy, and was easily being muscled off the puck in practice and during games. This wasn't the "AJ" coach Dufton was used to seeing, and he was concerned.

Back at home, Ange was also worried. Since being cut from the Olympics, it was obvious to her that Angela was suffering emotionally. Everywhere they went, she says, her partner was dogged by questions about her release. Friends, family, co-workers, teammates and even strangers on the street wanted to make Angela relive that horrible time in her life over and over again. Angela wanted desperately to forget about Calgary and get her life back on track. Her first step was to find out what had been ailing her—first at the Olympic training camp and now at home in Toronto.

Encouraged by both Ange and her coach, Angela finally went to the doctor. After a battery of tests and follow-up visits, she was diagnosed with Graves' disease, a common overactive thyroid condition, with symptoms that include dramatic weight loss and chronic fatigue. Left untreated, Graves can also lead to serious heart problems and even death. On doctor's orders, Angela started taking medication to improve the thyroid levels in her blood. After two weeks on the meds, she started to return to normal, and over the next few months her game also came around. Subsequent doctors' appointments and blood tests showed Angela's condition had gone into remission, which meant her thyroid problem was gone. "I don't know why they [the national team] weren't able to find out what was wrong and diagnose it," says Ken. "Once they were able to identify it, she rebounded and came back to become the same player that I knew very quickly."

This was the first time in 20-plus years of playing hockey that

Angela faced a medical scare that threatened her career. Although she had been injured before, it was never this devastating. Angela had never even broken a bone playing the game. She was always a little bigger than the other girls, which served to her advantage—especially during the body-checking days—but she also spent a lot of time in the gym. "When you're young, you're young. That's one thing," says Angela. "As I got older, I got introduced to training and I took that seriously."

For all intents and purposes, Angela could have easily played until her early 40s. Her skill and conditioning were still there, but she was at a different stage in her life. She had Ange, and their first child, Christian, was on the way. It was clear hockey was no longer Angela's top priority. She had other people for whom she had to think about and provide. It seemed Angela was finally ready to hang up her skates. That is, until an unexpected phone call from an old coach changed her plans —at least for the moment.

In the wake of the 1998 Olympics, Melody Davidson was named the head coach of Canada's Women's hockey team, which, in 1999, was set to compete for the Three Nations Cup on home soil in Montreal. This was the first time the women's national program had been reassembled since their shocking defeat in Nagano. The training camp, held in Caledon, Ontario, was full of all the usual suspects, including a number of the players who represented Canada at the Olympics. Forty-one in all were battling for spots and included among them was Angela, who swallowed her pride and accepted an invitation from Melody to try out for the team.

"It's unfortunate she didn't make the 1998 team, but we still felt she could contribute in our situation and we wanted to give her that opportunity," says Melody, who had coached Angela as an assistant at the 1994 world championships. "She could be a game breaker both on the score board and in the physical sense as well."

Unlike Calgary, Angela came into this training camp 100 percent healthy. Going into her first practice, Angela says it was tough returning to the fold. But she tried to put the past behind her and prove to everyone she could still compete at the game's highest level. Melody was confident Angela could move on and her message to the veteran forward was simple: "That was tough for you last year. Switch gears and let's go!" Angela took her coach's comments to heart and went to work. She knew this could be her last opportunity to play for Canada, and she was going to leave it all on the ice.

When Canada revealed its Three Nations Cup roster on October 21, 1999, six players from Canada's 1998 Olympic team were cut: goaltenders Manon Rheaume and Lesley Reddon, veteran defence-man Geraldine Heaney, and forwards Vicky Sunohara, Lori Dupuis and Kathy McCormack.[1] To everyone's surprise, among those to make it was no. 8. This was the same player who almost a year earlier had been called a "defensive liability" and someone who lacked character. So what changed? Angela was healthy. She was also a little older and perhaps ever more humble thanks to her very public release from the Olympic program. And although she may not have been the player she was in the early 1990s, the one who could dominate a game singlehandedly, Melody felt her team's chances of winning were greater with Angela in the line-up. This was definitely not a decision made on the coaches' part to pay service to one of the game's pioneers. "We don't have the opportunity in our program to pay homage to players," says Melody. "I thought she could help our team, period."

During the Three Nations Cup tournament, it appeared that Melody's hunch about Angela was wrong. She was played sparingly and didn't seem to have the offensive punch that once defined her game. A player of her stature could have easily started to whine about her diminished role and lack of ice time. Many argued that's why Shannon Miller cut Angela from the Olympic squad in the first place, because she wouldn't accept being just a regular role player. On the contrary, Angela was just that in 1999 and never complained once. She was a model player and teammate who did everything the coach asked of her. "She wasn't a distraction at all," says Melody. "She was a really good teammate. In the past, her play did the talking. But I remember she was more vocal and involved with everybody."

As the tournament progressed, Angela was struggling to focus. Although she was committed to helping her team win, her thoughts were back home in Toronto with Ange and their new son Christian, who was just five weeks old. Missing her family fiercely, she picked up the phone and called Ange with a decision she had been grappling with for a while. "My heart is not where it once was," Angela confessed to her partner. "I don't know if I'll get my heart back into it." Fighting back tears, Angela went on to tell Ange she was going to hang up her skates. "If that's what you want," replied Ange, "I'll be there for you."

As their conversation ended, Ange immediately started scrambling to find a way to Montreal. Christian was still a newborn, and she didn't want to travel alone for a five-hour drive. Her family was not local, and many of her and Angela's friends were participating in another hockey tournament. Luckily, Ange got a hold of Diane McIntyre, a long-time friend of the pair, who made the trip to Montreal with her. Thanks to Diane's speedy driving, they made it to the Maurice Richard Arena in time to see Canada take on the U.S. in the final. Meanwhile, in the Canadian locker room, Angela addressed her teammates and broke the news that this would be her last game in a Team Canada jersey. "I've had a great career," she said. "There just comes a time when you want to move on to other things, and that move-on time has come for me."[2] What happened next played out like a Hollywood script.

Going into the final, Canada had beaten the U.S. twice in round robin play. Both games were seesaw affairs, and the championship game continued that trend. Canada got off to a fast start by scoring on a power play just over a minute into the game. The U.S. countered and tied things up on a power play of their own. In the second period, Cammi Granato put the U.S. ahead, and they carried the lead into the third period. A wraparound goal by Canada's Tammy Lee Shewchuk sent things into overtime. Sudden death solved nothing, so next came the dreaded shootout: one skater, one goalie and a world of pressure.

All tournament long, Melody made her players work on their breakaway moves in a little game during practice that she called the "showdown." Each and every time, the winner of that game was none other than Angela. So when it came time to send out her first shooter, Melody looked down the bench and called out for her veteran star. The more than 2,000 fans in the Maurice Richard Arena were on their feet now. Angela skated to centre ice, pushed the puck forward and began to pick up speed. As she came face-to-face with U.S. netminder Sarah Tueting, Angela went to her backhand and flicked the puck into the top corner of the net. The pro-Canada crowd erupted in cheers. Ange and Diane were jumping in the air, screaming. Unaffected, little Christian lay fast asleep. Even the noise from the cheering crowd couldn't wake him.

Canadian goalie Kim St-Pierre then went on to stop all the American shooters she faced. Angela's goal stood as the winner in the 3–2 Canada victory. After Kim turned away the last shooter, the Canadian players poured off the bench, with gloves, sticks, and helmets thrown in the air. In the middle of this blissful group was Angela, arms raised in victory: a storybook ending to a storybook career.

CHAPTER 12

Hockey Mom

Even before Angela had thought about retiring from hockey, she and Ange had talked about having a family. About a year before Angela's retirement, the two settled into their current home in Richmond Hill, Ontario, and they felt the time was right. As Angela was still playing, it was decided that Ange would carry their first child. The couple searched for a sperm donor who had similar physical characteristics to Angela, and found him through an agency in Rochester, New York. After many early-morning trips to a clinic in downtown Toronto, Ange became pregnant through invitro fertilization. In October 1999, she gave birth to a boy, Christian James-McDonald, a hockey player, like his parents, who got his first taste of hockey as a five-week-old, watching his mom's final Three Nations Cup in Montreal. Naturally, he was just 18 months when he put on his first pair of skates.

As with every new family, parenthood was an adjustment—more so for Angela. The full-time athlete now had to find balance among her sports, career and family. Most of the early responsibilities for Christian fell to Ange. With this dynamic, Ange was in charge of discipline, where Angela—the big kid that she is—just wanted to have fun with her young son. "For Christian's first five years, I did most of the parenting," says Ange. "I took care of the home front, and Angela took care of everything else outside."

Ange points out that "everything else" didn't just include paying the bills and maintaining a career. Being Angela James also means countless hours volunteering as a coach, speaker and mentor, noble pursuits that can be taxing on a family dynamic. This was something Ange was made aware of from the beginning of their relationship: Angela told her she was a "busy person." But she is also a loyal person who wants to please everyone and has a hard time saying "no." "Angela does everything for the family even though she is pulled in 100 different directions," says Ange. "I don't know if people realize how much she does, and how it affects our family."

Christian out for a postgame lap with his mom.
He'd be happier with a pair of skates on.

Because Ange carried Christian, Angela was able to continue with the life she was used to when their first child arrived. Although her days of playing competitive hockey were coming to a close, she never left the game or lost her passion for it. Angela continued to play recreational hockey, often skating with former male junior players and also in lower tier women's leagues.

As her time with Team Canada ended, so too did her career in the COWHL. She retired from the Aeros, her last season coming in 1999–2000. By this time, there were just three teams afloat in the COWHL, and it merged with Quebec's elite women's league to become the National Women's Hockey League (NWHL). This league lasted nine years before folding in 2007. Many NWHL players joined new teams in the Canadian Women's Hockey League, which continues today, with teams in Quebec and Ontario. Annually, since 2008, the League has appropriately rewarded its leading scorer with the "Angela James Bowl."

In Angela's final year with the Aeros, she was still producing points and playing great hockey, even by Angela James' standard, with 22 goals and 44 points in 27 games. During the previous season, she was fourth among League scorers with 36 goals and 55 points and was named to the all-star team for the NWHL's western division—hardly the usual accomplishments for a player preparing to retire. More importantly, she was playing with many of her closest friends and Team Canada mates, including Geraldine Heaney, Cassie Campbell-Pascall, Cheryl Pounder and Amanda Benoit, as well as her friend and tour guide from Finland, Sari Krooks. Yet with the ache of the Olympics still in her heart and all the changes in her personal life, she knew it was time to say good-bye to competitive hockey and the league she had built over nearly two decades. "I was missing out on the best times with Christian," says Angela. "You have to give a little bit at home. You can't just play all the time."

And while Angela continued to play once or twice a week for fun in a Senior A "beer league," she found that she was often the centre of attention, but not in a good way. She was being hacked, slashed and provoked by less skilled players trying to make their marks and build their reputations by taking on the tough legend. Angela wasn't having any of it. She wanted to play, stay active and have fun, but being a target made her angry. "If you're going to make someone look stupid, they'll chop you down," she says. "I just wanted some exercise. I found that people were running me, on top of me. I didn't need it. I knew I'd start losing it, so I said 'That's it for me.'"

Angela would keep playing, but just for fun—she and Ange continued to skate in a weekly pick-up game with friends every Monday night at Seneca College. But in 2000, with her new son, and the hope for more children, Angela could see her priorities shifting; whereas hockey had been everything to her, she now had to balance that passion with motherhood.

Angela and Ange continued to enjoy the experience of raising Christian and saw a big shift in their lifestyle. Both have a lot of friends and were active in many ways, sports-related and otherwise. As moms, they understood quickly that time becomes a precious commodity, and a young child changes so quickly, so often, you never want to miss a moment. "It is a totally different direction now in our lives," says Angela. "Now, it's family and what's important for the kids. We had our time, we have done all these things, but it's not like we stopped living or anything."

When Christian was five, the two decided it was time to expand the family roster. This time, Angela would have the responsibility of carrying the child. This was a bit of a concern, considering Angela was now 40, and Ange wasn't sure how her always-on-the-move partner would adjust to being pregnant and having to slow down. Yet this was something Angela felt strongly about and wanted to experience. The couple wanted to use the same donor since Christian was such a handsome fellow—even the receptionist at the fertility clinic, on seeing a photo of the donor, insisted that he was a "must-have." The fertilization went as planned and Angela became pregnant in early 2004. What neither Angela nor Ange expected was that the family would not grow by one, but by two.

The news of twins was a happy surprise, although a bit of a scary one. How in the world would the moms handle two babies, along with Christian, not to mention maintain balance in their relationship and their careers? It would be much tougher for Angela. Being pregnant meant a big lifestyle change, although she continued to work at Seneca until she gave birth and was golfing and refereeing until her second trimester. There was one indulgence she was reluctant to give up until Christian set her straight.

"I started riding a motorcycle, right before I got pregnant—a Kawasaki Ninja," says Angela. "It's something I always wanted to do, but my mom wouldn't let me. The only reason I stopped was because Christian said, 'Mama, don't you think because you have two babies in your belly, you should stop riding your motorcycle?'"

It was good advice. As Angela remembers, she knew she would get big, but didn't realize she'd be "bursting." And when the time came, in November 2004, fraternal twins Toni and Michael were born. The constantly busy Angela James would experience a completely different kind of role on her family's team: sleep deprived, stay-at-home mom. She embraced it wholeheartedly, and it gave her a new appreciation for what Ange had gone through during the early days of Christian's life. "Looking back, [Angela carrying the twins] was the best thing for our relationship," says Ange. "For the first two months, Angela was breast feeding, being in there, doing everything."

Angela credits Ange for helping her understand the responsibility and diligence needed to run a successful household, especially one that includes three small children. Ange grew up on a farm, and chores were a part of her daily routine. Angela, the baby of her family and the star athlete, didn't have the same obligations. "Angela said she always hounded her sisters until they did the dishes," says Ange. "In the last five years that has changed." Ange has also instilled that responsibility in the kids. Christian learned how to cook when he was 10, and everybody—including the twins and their celebrity mom—pulls their own weight. "Ange made me change because she is all about family," says Angela. "That was tough because I kept cruising along, and I had to make sure that family was the number one priority on my list. It's all shifted now. The kids are number one."

In the years after the twins' birth, both Angela and Ange would be pulled in countless directions keeping up with their kids: hockey, swimming, soccer and many school activities. And although Angela's playing days were over, hockey was far from through with her. In the mid-2000s, the "hockey mom" would be pulled back into the spotlight, and whether she or Ange liked it or not, their lives would become a lot busier than either could have imagined.

Proud mom with twins Michael and Toni.

CHAPTER 13

Award Season

In the late 2000s, Linda Stapleton, Angela's mentor and friend from Seneca College, received a strange request from Barbados. They wanted to know if Angela had any Barbadian lineage. The small island country, where they don't really play hockey, wanted to claim her as its own. Angela couldn't really figure out why. It was a moot point, as Angela's family tree does not include any Barbadian branches. Although she was flattered, inquires like these confused Angela. "Sometimes I think, 'Do you guys really know the game? Do you know me?'" she says. "Just because I get one award or recognition, should I get another?"

Recognition was not a new phenomenon for Angela. She had been praised for her on-ice accomplishments on numerous occasions, dating back to her days in youth hockey. Off-ice recognition also came often. In 1985, she was named Toronto's Youth of the Year (an award sadly lost when the family was evicted from Graydon Hall), and in 1992, she received the Women in Sport Enhancement Award, also from the City of Toronto. Yet it was after Angela's retirement when the accolades really began to roll in.

In 2001, Seneca College retired her no. 8 jersey and immortalized her accomplishments with a plaque containing photos of her and a glass-encased display, with memorabilia and statistics from her career, at the Seneca Sports Centre. Scripted on the display are the words, "Simply the best." This tribute takes into account a relationship with Seneca that started when Angela was just a teenager and has lasted more than 30 years.

The College also recognized her with its prestigious Distinguished Alumni Award, and she's been a two-time nominee for the Ontario Premier's Award for College Graduates. Angela has become synonymous with Seneca in many ways: as a student, athlete and employee. "I really think she feels respected here," says Linda. "She feels like a part of the family, and I think she's been an inspiration to our staff and students."

The many athletes who followed in Angela's footsteps in collegiate sports and amateur hockey have been inspired by her accomplishments, as has been demonstrated by her continuous appeal as a mentor and coach. When her playing days ended, she served as head coach for Ontario's 2001 gold-medal-winning under-18 national championship team. She has also spent years coaching girls teams across Ontario. Often parents would find out where she was coaching and try to get their girls on Angela's teams. "They all know her story," said Steve Redding, one of Angela's co-coaches on a pee-wee team she led in North York. "And for many of them she has been an idol since they can remember. She has forgotten more about hockey than I will ever know."[1]

In 2005, Angela's ongoing impact on women's hockey in Canada was recognized with Hockey Canada's Female Hockey Breakthrough award. This award is given to those who demonstrate leadership and contribute to the advancement of the game for girls and women in Canada. Considering Angela's ongoing dedication to hockey as a player, coach, official and ambassador, it was as though this award was designed for her.

With all her accomplishments as a player, and later as a coach, it is easy to overlook that Angela is an elite (level four) referee, who was a referee-in-chief for the Ontario Women's Hockey Association. Funnily enough, as a referee, Angela became a piece of infamous women's hockey history.

In 1986, while she was officiating a provincial championship in Mississauga, Ontario, a player named Trudy Banwell became so enraged with a high-sticking penalty that she charged at Angela, knocking her to the ice. Trudy then turned her sights on the linesman, Barb Jeffery, attacked her, and separated Barb's shoulder. As a result of the incident, Trudy became the first-ever Canadian female hockey player to be convicted of assault. She was given a conditional discharge and two years' probation.[2] "I remember every single bit of that. I had to go to court," says Angela. "The girl went berserk. Then the other linesman, who was a guy, grabbed [Trudy], then the coach came off the bench and started punching the linesman. Total havoc."

Happily, that incident did not turn Angela off refereeing. She's been doing it for more than 20 years; it was one of the ways she supported herself during her studies and something she still enjoys today, for exercise and maintaining a connection to the game at ice level. And she hasn't been attacked since.

Along with the Breakthrough award, 2005 also brought Angela's induction in the Ontario College Athletic Association's Hall of Fame. This award was no surprise, considering Angela's unbelievable college career on the ice and the softball diamond. The OCAA called her "one of the top players of her era."

Now the stuff of legend, Angela's list of college accomplishments is staggering: three-time OCAA scoring leader, including a 50 goal season in 1984–85—as a defenceman; OCAA Women's Hockey MVP for three consecutive years; a two-time OCAA All-Star; and the OCAA's all-time leading scorer. In softball, she led the Seneca Scouts to the inaugural OCAA women's championship in 1982 and was named an OCAA All-Star.

It was clear Angela was ahead of her time as an Ontario college hockey player with regard to the level of collegiate competition in the province—and four years of seasoning in the COWHL didn't hurt either. Angela was a force of nature at Seneca, and she recalls her college days as one of the happiest periods of her life. The effects of her play still resonate, as her 2005 OCAA Hall of Fame induction demonstrated. "People stopped what they were doing and watched her," says Linda. "You just knew you were in the presence of great-ness."

During her college days and into adulthood, it became clear to Angela that she was different on the ice, not just in terms of her ability, but also because of the colour of her skin; she did not see any significant level of racial diversity during her playing days. Although this has changed in recent years, with young people of all backgrounds taking up the game, Angela came to the realization that she was one of the few minority players in hockey. There were a handful of ugly incidents in which her race was brought to the forefront by her opponents as means of goading Angela, and she responded appropriately—with her fists or a booming hit. Yet her race was never a significant issue for her or her teammates. Angela's heritage is a source of pride for her, which made what happened in 2007 extra special.

In February of that year, Angela was notified that she was being inducted into the Black Ice Hockey and Sports Hall of Fame. The Hall, which is located in Dartmouth, Nova Scotia, was honouring its second-ever class of teams and players. Angela was one of eight players inducted, along with some of the pioneers of what was called "the Coloured Hockey League," which operated in Eastern Canada at the turn of the century. Also inducted that year were NHL goaltenders Ray Emery and Eldon "Pokey" Reddick.

The Black Ice Hockey and Sports Hall of Fame is part of the Black Ice Project, which was created in 2004 by the Stryker-Indigo Publishing Company, Inc. of New York. The project promotes social responsibility, historic preservation, religious tolerance and societal non-violence through hockey and its history. Each year, the Hall hosts conferences to celebrate black athletes and their roles in North American Society.[3] These conferences also contextualize the important role that black men and women have played in reshaping American and Canadian sporting cultures.

Going to Nova Scotia allowed Angela to reflect on her own roots and learn more about the rich history of the many black hockey players from Eastern Canada. Canadian sports historian Bill Humber, in his retrospective of African-Canadian sporting achievements, A Sporting Chance, describes how hockey was "an early attempt by the black community in Canada to use sports as a means of intentionally connecting with the country's emerging self-identity."[4] "The trip

140

to Nova Scotia was intriguing for me," says Angela. "I never paid much attention to my cultural history until then. Many of the black people living in Eastern Canada were playing before anyone else in Canada."

Upon her induction, Angela probably thought about Jennifer Neil, a mixed-race hockey player, who, when she was 14, wrote a poem to Angela, her idol and inspiration. Jennifer first saw Angela at the national team training camp in 1994. Watching her on the ice, Jennifer told some friends, "I wish I could be like that." Later, Jennifer said that after meeting Angela, she decided to stay with hockey—something she would not have done otherwise. "Something clicked in me," said Jennifer. "I wanted to set a goal for myself. The way she skated, her shot. She's awesome [...] Nothing will stop her."[5] Nothing stopped Jennifer either. She continued a successful hockey career, first with Angela's Toronto Aeros, and then as a student-athlete at Princeton University.

Although the awards continued to pile up, Angela contends that these kinds of "lifetime recognition" honours were unimportant to her. She found that only when the media got on board and gave her a call did she begin thinking about the possibility of a given award. This was the case with the International Ice Hockey Hall of Fame and the Canada's Sports Hall of Fame. Both were complete shocks for her when she found out she was going to be inducted, in 2008 and 2009, respectively. "It's not something I thought would happen," she says. "It was not what I was playing for."

Angela made no bones about the fact that winning was always her number-one goal. Championships were her definition of success. Whether she thought about it or not, recognition is often a by-product of success. Even though it had been almost a decade since her retirement, Angela's accomplishments still held significance with the international and Canadian hockey communities. The International Ice Hockey Federation induction, like the Hockey Hall of Fame induction that would follow, was groundbreaking because it marked the first time a woman would be recognized in the IIHF Hall. It was made even sweeter because Angela would be joined by Geraldine Heaney, as well as her former adversary from the United States, Cammi Granato.

Their induction was a victory for Hockey Canada as well. Executives had been lobbying to bring down the gender barrier when it came to career recognition in hockey's premier governing institutions, like the IIHF. "I had been pushing this for a long time," says Hockey Canada President Bob Nicholson. "We nominated both [Angela and Geraldine]. To me, the IIHF made the right decision."

Angela poses with her fellow IIHF Hall of Fame inductees (top row, left to right): Walter L. Bush Jr., Chair of the IIHF Selection Committee; Juraj Okolicany; Phillippe Bozon; Art Berglund; Igor Larionov; (bottom row, left to right): Angela; Cammi Granato; and Geraldine Heaney.

Angela holds her IIHF Fall of Fame induction plaque.

Angela and Linda Stapleton at Angela's induction to Canada's Sports
Hall of Fame.

Angela and Geraldine became two of the only 13 Canadians in the IIHF Hall of Fame. They were welcomed in Quebec City as the IIHF celebrated its 100th anniversary. Joining them was NHL legend Mario Lemieux; the ageless Russian wonder Igor Larionov, a standout in the Soviet Union before joining the NHL and leading the Detroit Red Wings to three Stanley Cups; and the first-ever NHL player born in France, Philippe Bozon.

Geraldine dedicated her induction to her late sister, Catherine, who had died of cancer two weeks prior to the ceremony in May, 2008. Angela called their induction a building block for the future of the sport. "It's not a female or male sport," she said at the time. "It's hockey. It's our game."[6] For Angela, one of the highlights of the induction was playing in the commemorative game with Larionov, two-time Conn Smythe trophy winner Patrick Roy, and celebrities like Jim Balsillie—the former co-CEO of Research in Motion, maker of the Blackberry. The best part, by far, though, was having Christian on the bench "coaching" the roster of superstars.

For some—including Cassie Campbell-Pascall, who was inducted a year earlier—Angela's next major recognition by Canada's Sports Hall of Fame in 2009 was a little slow in coming. Cassie had dedicated her induction to Angela. "I felt uncomfortable being in there before Angela," she says. "I didn't deserve that before her. But I guess people don't know the history." Cassie served on Canada's Sports Hall of Fame selection board the following year and made clear her case for what she called Angela's "no-brainer" induction. She certainly made her point.

Upon her induction, Angela was lauded as a "pioneer, made of tough stuff, and one of Canada's greatest female hockey players." The term pioneer makes Angela feel uneasy ("When I think pioneer, I think old and grey," she says), but another term the Sports Hall used to describe her was "champion." The induction recognized her history of winning for Canada, and how she became a role model in her community and across the country.

Earlier in 2009, Angela was also honoured with arguably the most significant and appropriate testament to her career, her impact as an athlete, and as a role model. This development began close to home, and was driven by one of Angela's biggest fans—her sister Kym. Kym approached Andrew Fairbain, a friend from Angela's ball hockey days, and Toronto Councillor John Parker, about re-naming the Flemingdon Park Arena, "the Angela James Arena." Councillor Parker presented the request to be voted upon at Toronto City Hall, and it was a unanimous decision: the building where Angela had first played the game that would come to define her would now bear her name.

Not that there wasn't some irony attached to this honour: Angela was not always welcome at the Flemingdon Park Arena, where, as an eight-year-old, she was told she couldn't play with the boys. Now Angela was a returning hero, the ultimate example of "local kid makes good." But this kid had made more than good: she had helped to define a sport and changed the way people saw what women could do on the ice. Now every child in eastern Toronto, regardless of gender or race, who wishes to learn the game of hockey, can do so without prejudice or judgment at the Angela James Arena.

On a sunny afternoon in June, 2009, Angela, surrounded by her family, hosted a community barbecue to announce the renaming of the arena. She thanked her mother, her siblings, Ange, and their children, for their ongoing love and support. She also recalled the countless hours she spent in the Park, playing, watching, learning and falling in love with hockey. All that she achieved and became began there. It was home.

"The naming of the arena touched me the most of all the awards," says Angela. "It's something so personal to me and my family. It was where I was brought up, where I learned to play the game, where all the stories I tell come from. It was really overwhelming and a nice ceremony. It felt like being back at the old Park again. The new sign could have been just a piece of paper and I would have felt the same."

Angela now jokes that she gets emails from people asking where her arena is, not that she is complaining. This public recognition, along with all of the inductions and honours bestowed upon her throughout the decade, were thrilling and humbling for Angela and her family. Yet as touched as she was by the arena naming and the awards that had preceded it, compared to what happened the following June, it all would seem like a pregame skate.

On the fateful afternoon of June 22, 2010, while Angela was at home in Richmond Hill with Ange, she got the phone call she never imagined would come; the call that, when she started playing as a girl without a league and when her Olympic dream was crushed, was not even conceivable. Those disappointments, not to mention all the hard work, the championships, the goals and the scars were now simply prologue. The call had come. And on the other end of the line was the Hockey Hall of Fame, inviting her to hockey's biggest night.

CHAPTER 14

Induction Day

The cameras were flashing as the who's who of the hockey world made their way down the red carpet into the Great Hall of the Hockey Hall of Fame in downtown Toronto. Inside the hockey cathedral the guests started to take their seats for an historic night. Sitting in the front row was Angela, with Ange and their children. Directly behind them sat Angela's family—brother Bobby, sisters Kym and Cindy, her mother Donna and even her estranged father, Leo. Also in attendance were members of Ange's family, who flew in from Prince Edward Island for this special night.

All week long, the Hockey Hall of Fame and its committee held events to celebrate its newest members. There were autograph signings and forums, a ceremonial puck drop at the Air Canada Centre, a Legends Game, and a presentation of the inductees Hockey Hall of Fame jackets and member rings. At the Legends Game, Angela took to the ice with former NHL stars and scored a beautiful goal on a goal crease pass from fellow Hall of Famer Glenn Anderson.

The Sunday afternoon of the Legends Game, the Air Canada Centre was awash with young female hockey players in colourful jerseys, from teams across Ontario—cities like Barrie, Orangeville and Oakville. All were there for one reason: to see Angela James. Also in the stands were women of all ages, decked out in Team Canada jerseys, celebrating a piece of history. One woman, named Connie Ross, had been a supporter of women's hockey since the 1970s, and was thrown back to her childhood in this setting. Seeing the Hockey Hall of Fame induct its first women made her think of her mother and their common passion for the game. "There are a lot of moms and daughters here today, which is really impressive," she said. "It's a family game. Even women my age are still playing and picking up the sport now. Everybody can enjoy it."

After the full schedule of commemorative events, the only thing that remained was the official ceremony to welcome the 2010 inductees. The class of 2010 included long-time Detroit Red Wings executive Jimmy Devellano; the late Daryl "Doc" Seaman, a founding owner of the Calgary Flames; and Dino Ciccarelli, a 600-plus goal scorer and veteran of more than 1,200 NHL games.

Joining these accomplished male greats were the first two women ever inducted into the Hockey Hall of Fame: Cammi Granato and Angela James. Cammi was a 15-year member of the U.S. Women's National team who captained her country to the gold medal in the 1998 Winter Olympics, and to this day she remains the all-time leader in goals and points for the Americans in world championships. Angela was the best female player in the world in the 1980s and 1990s, and her list of accomplishments is without comparison among her contemporaries. It was clear her rightful place was among hockey's biggest stars in the Hall of Fame, and on Monday, November 8, 2010, the first superstar of women's hockey blazed yet another trail for her peers to follow.

More than 2,000 people were seated in the Great Hall waiting to hear the acceptance speeches of the newest inductees. The first to take the stage was the hometown girl. All week long, Angela had been speaking first at each Hockey Hall of Fame event, and on this night there would be no exception. Admittedly nervous, Angela's fears subsided for the moment when a video was played highlighting her career accomplishments. The five-minute vignette featured a young Angela James growing up in Flemingdon Park and her journey from playing boy's hockey to joining the COWHL as a 13-year-old. There were images of her holding countless MVP and championship trophies and highlight reel goals from her time with Team Canada.

Friends like Hayley Wickenheiser and Cassie Campbell-Pascall talked about what made Angela the special player she was and her immeasurable contributions to the game. Once the video ended, the room erupted into applause as Angela was called up to the stage to accept her Honoured Members plaque from Hockey Hall of Fame Chairman and CEO Bill Hay.

Smiling and shaking her head in utter disbelief, Angela walked to the podium, looked out at the audience and said, "You know this has been a long-time coming. I need to turn around and take a look at this." Directly behind Angela stood a large multi-coloured arch with all the names of the inductees and the official members' logo. "James" was the first name on this impressive list of hockey legends. Angela looked up at her name in lights, raised her hands and began pumping them up in the air in celebration. Her gesture drew cheers from the crowd and helped to ease some of the butterflies.

Angela stepped back to the microphone and started her speech by thanking the Hockey Hall of Fame committee and its staff for bestowing this honour on her, and for the first-class hospitality that was shown to her family throughout the week. "The limo ride alone, we could go home and that would be the end of it," joked Angela. The audience laughed, and she continued to keep her speech light, likening the Hockey Hall of Fame to a family into which she felt adopted. It was a family of boys, which, of course, "needed some girls," Angela said with a big, devilish grin on her face.

After a few more icebreaking remarks, Angela started to get reflective. She told the audience that she never thought the game of hockey was only for boys. She talked about how she discovered the game as a kid growing up in Flemingdon Park, where she skated and played hockey until the lights went out at her neighbourhood rink. During the non-winter months, she would switch to street hockey, perfecting her famous slap shot by hammering a tennis ball up against the wall over and over again until she couldn't see anymore.

"Hockey is what I did," said Angela, "and still do to this very day." She credited the game for keeping her out of trouble and away from the dangers that surrounded her childhood. But she didn't do it alone and was sure to credit the many coaches, co-workers, friends and former players who guided her along the way. She sent out a special thank you to her best friend, Carol Law, who took it upon herself to protect a young, up-and-coming child who made the jump to the women's senior league.

Angela thanked her Team Canada teammates and life-long friends Cathy Phillips and Geraldine Heaney. For a time, this dynamic trio was considered the best power forward, goalie and defenceman playing in the women's game. Together, they delivered Canada's first world championship in 1990, dominating the competition in what was only a small sign of things to come. Angela went on to thank her coaches. She mentioned Ken Dufton and Colin MacKenzie from the Toronto Aeros organization. Both men approached women's hockey professionally and provided the players on their team with the resources they needed to be successful, including more practice time, better equipment and the best coaching staff in the league.

Under Ken's coaching, Angela became a complete player and the most dominant force in the COWHL. Angela also thanked her college coach Lee Trempe for guiding her on and off the ice. Thanks to Lee, Mary Zettel, who originally recruited no. 8 to Seneca, and Linda Stapleton, Angela earned a college diploma and developed a career. She has been employed at Seneca since her graduation, now serving as the Senior Recreation Coordinator, responsible for developing and delivering the same types of sports and recreation programs that helped her to achieve her dreams. "Without these people, I would have never completed this journey," said Angela.

Angela also recognized the builders of the women's game, specifically praising Fran Rider and Bob Nicholson for helping foster the game at home and abroad. The hardest part of her speech, however, came next, as Angela looked out into the front row and started thanking her family members—that cast of characters who helped a little girl achieve her ice dreams.

There were her brothers, Bobby and Larry, who each played the sport and encouraged their kid sister to follow suit, despite the fact that she was a girl. There was Cindy, Angela's big sister and "second mom," whom she would fight with every Saturday night to stay up and watch Hockey Night in Canada. Sitting beside Cindy in the audience was Kym, Angela's partner in crime back in their Flemingdon

Park days. Despite all her personal struggles, Kym was always there for her, dragging Angela and her bags to games on public transit or by foot—whatever it took to get her on the ice. Angela also thanked her dad Leo: "No matter what, if I called you," she said, "you would be there."

As Angela looked down at the next name on her list, she started to choke up. The tears filling her big, brown eyes were for her mother, Donna, the single parent of five children who had no money to her name but always managed to provide her kids with everything they needed, especially her youngest. In that moment, the family's struggles came racing back to Angela, who never in her wildest dreams thought she'd be standing on the stage of the Hockey Hall of Fame, giving a speech on the occasion of her induction. She had a lot of people to thank for her remarkable Cinderella story, but none were more influential to her success than the little lady with the grey hair, sitting in the second row, still the ever-proud hockey mom. "My Mum," said Angela, her voice cracking. "My lovely Mum. You always found a way to allow me to play no matter what happened or where you were."

The emotion in Angela's speech continued to build as she talked about her own family. Even though it was well past their bedtime, all the kids were still up, except for Toni who had fallen sound asleep in Ange's arms. Michael, the family's natural born comedian, was sitting on the floor, playing with Cammi Granato's little boy, while Christian sat in his own seat following his mother's every word. When Angela finally mentioned her eldest by name, he did a double pump in the air that brought an immediate grin to Angela's face. What came next was by far the most poignant moment of the evening.

As Angela thanked her partner of 16 years and their three children, cameras broadcasting the induction live zoomed in on the hockey legend's family. The camera cut back to Angela as she told the audience, "They were the ones who made the sacrifices night after night to allow me to play this game." I know you might not understand now," said Angela looking at her children. "But tonight your mom has climbed a very tall mountain."

The newest hall of famer receives her ring from (left to right) Bill Hay and Jim Gregory.

Angela with her long time friend and teammate Fran Rider at Angela's Hockey Hall of Fame induction.

Hockey Hall of Fame, class of 2010: (left to right) Jimmy Devellano, Angela, Dino Ciccarelli, Cammi Granato and Bob Seaman, representing Daryl K. "Doc" Seaman.

Angela and Christian surrounded by the greats at the Hockey Hall of Fame.

CHAPTER 15

The Reluctant Pioneer

In the days following her induction, Angela was flooded with media requests. But it wasn't just sports writers calling, the Lesbian, Gay, Bisexual and Transgender (LGBT) community also wanted desperately to talk to the new Hall of Famer. Although Angela had always been open about her sexuality, many people inside and outside of the game found out for the first time that she was gay on the night of her induction. For the LGBT community, this was a significant development, considering no openly gay athlete had ever been inducted into any of the major league sports halls of fame in North America.

The LGBT media in Canada and abroad jumped on the story and began writing about Angela and her hockey accomplishments. Many of their readers had no idea who Angela James was, but that didn't stop them from inundating online forums with congratulatory messages after reading her story. They commended her for her bravery to live an open life. Unexpectedly, these were the same types of responses Angela heard the night of her induction, when she thanked Ange in her speech. Even within the often homophobic hockey world, current and former players, coaches and executives came up to Angela and applauded her for recognizing her life partner. Only after the ceremony, however, did Angela realize how monumental her speech was.

Despite the progress society has made to accept members of the LGBT community, in the world of sports—especially hockey—being gay is still very much a taboo. To date, no current or former NHL player has "come out." Angela, for one, can't wait for the day when gay athletes can be themselves and express who they are openly, without any fear of consequences. "I think it's important that we be who we are," says Angela. "I am who I am, and I'm proud."

Never forgetting who she is and where she came from is truly at the heart of Angela's success in hockey, and in life. The mountain she climbed to get into the Hall was indeed high and full of barriers that many of the other inductees never faced. In addition to being the first gay athlete and first Canadian woman inducted into the Hall, Angela also became only the second black player to be enshrined. Grant Fuhr, the outstanding Edmonton Oilers goaltender, was the first in 2003.

Skin colour and sexual orientation aside, the induction of Angela James into the Hockey Hall of Fame has charted a course for others to follow. With its decision to evaluate women and men separately, the Hall has promised the list of female inductees will grow in the future. Hayley Wickenheiser, who has now emerged as the greatest female hockey player, is the next logical choice for induction—when she decides to retire. When her time comes, she will be standing on the shoulders of the players, like Angela, who blazed the trail. "She [Angela] led the women's game into a new era," says Hayley. "She brought a presence, a professionalism to the game, set a standard and wouldn't accept less than the best."

Hayley's sentiments are shared by many of those who know the women's game best and strongly believe Angela is responsible for increasing the visibility of women's hockey, especially in Canada. "She is a women's hockey hero who continues to inspire young players across the country," says Bob Nicholson, one of the architects of the women's national program in Canada. "For me, she will always be the Wayne Gretzky of women's hockey."

Fran Rider believes all the work of the game's volunteers, players, coaches, sponsors and administrators would have been for nothing if, at the end of the day, the product on the ice "wasn't any good." "A lot of the credibility came from AJ's ability," says Fran. "As we developed teams throughout Ontario and contacts throughout Canada, the U.S. and the rest of the world, AJ's name became the name that was known." Without Angela James, Fran also argues that the International Olympic Committee would not have recognized women's hockey as an official Olympic sport. "The fact is we wouldn't be there if it hadn't been for her: none of us."

Melody Davidson, the coach of Canada's 2010 gold-medal-winning Olympic team, credits Angela for inspiring young girls around the world to play the game. "Angela was like so many veteran players. They've trail-blazed, knocked down obstacles to open doors for young girls," she says. "The reason that young girls get the opportunity to play is because of players like Angela James. So many things that she did through the early 1980s and 1990s led the way to where we are right now, and where we are going in the future."

The future of the women's game has never been brighter, and one has to look no further than the Angela James Arena to see its popularity. During the hockey season, this building is buzzing with parents taking their children to practices and games. Unlike when Angela first played there, it's no longer an all-boys club. There are girls of all ages on the ice—many of whom are aspiring to be the next Angela James. The best part is, they are playing right alongside the boys, and no one is telling them they have to leave.

With young girls and women's league participation numbers at a record high in Canada, it seems it's only a matter of time before women will have a professional hockey league to call their own. The Canadian Women's Hockey League (CWHL), for example, is piloting a professional league with teams based in Toronto, Brampton, Burlington, Montreal, and Boston. The CWHL held an official draft and players were selected from around the world, including Canada, the U.S., Slovenia, Sweden, Switzerland, Finland, Germany and Russia. Angela was even hired to coach the Brampton team before stepping down due to family commitments. The CWHL's ultimate goal, however, is to receive official endorsement from the NHL—similar to the National Basketball Association's financial support and development of the Women's National Basketball Association, which launched in 1996 and still operates today.

That there is even a discussion taking place about the possibility of an NHL-sponsored women's hockey league brings an immediate smile to Angela's face. During her hockey career, she was never paid to play. Angela went to work, rushed home to grab dinner and then went straight to the arena. The next day, she would wake up and do it all over again. For girls like Angela who dared to pick up a hockey stick and lace up a pair of skates, the goal was not fame or fortune; they just wanted to play the game they loved.

From the earliest days of her childhood, Angela James developed a love affair with Canada's national pastime that remains strong to this day. Even at 46, she still takes to the ice regularly with Ange and their friends. Yet, her primary hockey focus for the foreseeable future will be on her kids and helping them to develop as players and as people. Even if none of them follow in their mother's footsteps, Angela doesn't care. She just wants her children to have direction. "Ange and I definitely want them to get an education," she says. "And we just want them to be good people and good members of society."

Although the term "pioneer" makes her feel old, considering the remarkable journey she took to get into the Hockey Hall of Fame that's exactly what Angela is. With the undying devotion of her mother, siblings, friends, teammates and life partner, she led the long and arduous climb to bring national prominence and international success to women's hockey. Her rise to stardom was a long shot, but her unparalleled talent, dedication and intensity made her an elite player and the first superstar of the women's game. Her story is proof to young girls and boys everywhere that you can always change your destiny when you devote yourself to a dream. "My roots are Flemingdon Park, but it doesn't mean what we were exposed to was how we had to live in the future," says Angela. "You can never forget where you come from, but you can always change where you're going."

The James-McDonald family pays a visit to Santa (left to right):
Christian; Michael; Angela; Ange and Toni.

AWARDS AND HONOURS

- YWCA Women of Distinction award (2012)

- One of the first two women inducted into the Hockey Hall of Fame (2010)

- Two-time nominee for the Ontario Premier's Award for College Graduates (2010, 1994)

- Inducted into Canada's Sports Hall of Fame (2009)

- Flemingdon Park Arena renamed the Angela James Arena (2009)

- One of the first three women inducted into the International Ice Hockey Federation Hall of Fame (2008)

- "The Angela James Bowl" is established to honour the Canadian Women's Hockey League's top scorer (2008)

- Inducted into the Ontario Ball Hockey Association Hall of Fame (2007)

- Inducted into the Black Ice Hockey and Sports Hall of Fame (2006)

- Inducted into the Ontario College Athletics Association Hall of Fame (2006)

- Seneca College Distinguished Alumni Award winner (2003)

- Women in Sport Enhancement, City of Toronto (1992)

- Three-time Seneca College Female Varsity Athlete of the Year

- Youth of the Year Award, City of Toronto (1985)

ANGELA JAMES

CAREER INTERNATIONAL TOURNAMENT STATISTICS: TEAM CANADA

Season	Club	League	GP	G	A	TP	PIM
1982-1983	Seneca College	OCAA	8	15	10	25	
1983-1984	Seneca College	OCAA	10	15	15	30	
1984-1985	Seneca College	OCAA	14	50	23	73	10
1989-1990	Canada	WWC	5	11	2	13	2
1991-1992	Canada	WWC	5	5	2	7	67
1992-1993	Toronto Aeros	COWHL	23	16	19	34	2
1993-1994	Canada	WWC	5	4	5	9	41
1993-1994	Toronto Aeros	COWHL	28	30	40	70	2
1995-1996	Canada	Pacific Rim	5	3	4	7	2
1995-1996	Canada	3 Nations	5	1	2	3	2
1995-1996	Toronto Red Wings	COWHL	29	35	35	70	37
1996-1997	Newtonbrook Panthers	COWHL	28	29	29	58	57
1996-1997	Canada	WWC	5	2	3	5	2
1997-1998	Toronto Aeros	COWHL	9	6	3	9	19
1997-1998	Canada	Nat-Team	15	7	1	8	4
1998-1999	North York/Beatrice Aeros	NWHL	31	36	19	55	30
1998-1999	Canada	3 Nations	3	0	2	2	0
1999-2000	Canada	3 Nations	2	0	0	0	0
1999-2000	North York/Beatrice Aeros	NWHL	27	22	22	44	10
TOTALS			257	287	236	522	285

Source: Hockey Hall of Fame

PHOTO CREDITS

Foreword
Adam Graves: Tom Bartsiokas
Flemingdon Kings Photo: Adam Graves

Chapter 2
Angela and Cindy: Angela James

Chapter 3
Angela and Kym: Angela James
Flemingdon Family photo: Angela James

Chapter 4
Angela in her Flemingdon Park hockey uniform: Angela James

Chapter 5
Angela in her softball uniform: Seneca College
Angela rounds second during a softball game: Angela James
Seneca Scouts group shot: Seneca College

Chapter 6
Angela playing for Mark's Diesels: Angela James
Team Ontario, 1987: Angela James

Chapter 8
Angela on Team Canada: Angela James
1992 Team Canada: Angela James

Chapter 9
Angela and Ange in their early days: Angela James

Chapter 12
Christian and Mom on the ice: Angela James
Angela and her new twins: Angela James

Chapter 13
Angela poses with her fellow IIHF Hall of Fame inductees: HHOF/
IIHF Images
Angela holds her IIHF Hall of Fame induction plaque: HHOF/
IIHF Images
Angela and Linda Stapleton at Angela's induction to Canada's Sports
Hall of Fame: Angela James

Chapter 14
Angela with Bill Hay and Jim Gregory: Tom Bartsiokas
Angela and Fran Rider at Hockey Hall of Fame induction: HHOF/
IIHF Images
Hockey Hall of Fame, class of 2010: Tom Bartsiokas
Angela and Christian at the Hockey Hall of Fame: Tom Bartsiokas

Chapter 15
The James-McDonald family meets Santa: Angela James

NOTES

Chapter 1
1. Robin Brown, Interview, 2010
2. Duhatschek: 1

Chapter 2
1. "Peckham salutes sister Angela James."

Chapter 3
1. "Flemingdon's great design": 1
2. Etue & Williams: 236

Chapter 4
1. Russell: 146
2. Russell: 146
3. Russell: 147
4. Russell: 147
5. Russell: 147
6. Avery & Stevens: 227

Chapter 5
1. "Three Senecans": 45

Chapter 6
1. Etue & Williams: 81
2. Etue & Williams: 240
3. Russell: 151

Chapter 7
1. Etue & Williams: 16
2. Schultz-Nicholson: 40
3. Schultz-Nicholson: 44
4. Schultz-Nicholson: 47
5. McFarlane: 152
6. McFarlane: 154

7. McFarlane: 151
8. McFarlane: 156
9. McFarlane: 155
10. Etue & Williams: 36

Chapter 8
1. McFarlane: 161
2. McFarlane: 162
3. Beacon: D1
4. McFarlane: 166
5. Russell: 158

Chapter 9
1. Cox: 1
2. Etue & Williams: 257
3. Cox: 1
4. Avery & Stevens: 232
5. Russell: 160
6. Avery & Stevens: 236
7. Russell: 161

Chapter 10
1. Maki: P2
2. Paul: P18
3. Warmington: 115
4. Warmington: 115
5. Warmington: 115
6. Warmington: 115
7. Warmington: 115
8. Christie: S1
9. Wright
10. Blatchford: 5
11. Paul: 141
12. "Disappointed James:" A25
13. "Disappointed James:" A25
14. "Disappointed James:" A25

15. Wright

Chapter 11
1. Buffery: P120
2. Russell: 139

Chapter 13
1. Russell: 132
2. McFarlane: 142
3. "The Black Ice Project"
4. Humber: 101
5. Etue & Williams: 265
6. "Hockey player:" B12

Chapter 14
James "Hockey Hall of Fame Speech"

Chapter 15
James "Hockey Hall of Fame Speech"

WORKS CITED

Avery, Joanna & Julie Stevens. *Too Many Men on the Ice: Women's Hockey in North America*. Victoria: Polestar, 1997.

Blatchford, Christie. "Frankly, Gay Rumors a Bust." *Toronto Sun*, February 6, 1998, sec. news, p. 5.

Beacon, Bill. "Canadian women win another world title." *The Globe and Mail*, April 18, 1994, sec. sports, p. D1

Buffery, Steve. "Three Nations Roster Shocker." *Toronto Sun*, October 22, 1999, sec. sports, p. 120.

Christie, James. "Controversy Checks Olympic Team Veteran of Women's Hockey Squad Fights Dismissal, Claim of Staff-player Relationship Surfaces." *The Globe and Mail*, December 19, 1997, sec. sports, p. S1.

Cox, Damian. "Canadian Women Begin Quest for Olympic Gold." *The Toronto Star Online*. October 15, 1996, URL: http://www.thestar.com/thestar/editorial/sports/961015SPB5_SP-COX15.html. [07.10.10]

Christie, James. "Disappointed James Won't Rule Out Appeal Women's 'Gretzky' Queries Being Labelled Defensive Liability; CHA Head Says Decision Fair." *The Globe and Mail*, December 20, 1997, sec. sports, p. A25.

Duhatschek, Eric. "The Case for Cassie." *The Globe and Mail Online*. September 5, 2007.URL: http://www.theglobeandmail.com/sports/hockey/globe-on-hockey/duhatschek-the-case-for-cassie/article757020/ [06.03.11]

Etue, Elizabeth & Megan K. Williams. *On the Edge: Women Making Hockey History*. Toronto: Second Story Press, 1996.

"Flemingdon's Great Design: $200 Million Development." *Toronto Daily Star,* January 19, 1966, Metro Edition.

"Hockey Players Make History." *St. John's Telegraph-Journal,* May 16, 2008, sec. sports, p. B12.

Humber, William. *A Sporting Chance: Achievements of African Canadian Athletes.* Toronto: Natural Heritage, 2004.

Ireland, Joanne. "Peckham salutes sister Angela James." Edmonton Journal Online. November 9, 2010, URL: http://blogs.edmontonjournal.com/2010/11/09/peckham-salutes-sister-angela-james/

James, Angela, "Hockey Hall of Fame Speech" (acceptance speech, Hockey Hall of Fame 2010 Induction Ceremony, Toronto, Canada, November 8, 2010).

Maki, Allan. "Olympic Coach Stands Tough on Move to Cut James." *The Globe and Mail,* December 10, 1997, sec. sports, p. 2.

McFarlane, Brian. *Proud Past, Bright Future: One Hundred Years of Canadian Women's Hockey.* Toronto: Stoddart, 1994.

Nicholson, Lorna Schultz. *Pink Power: The First Women's Hockey World Champions:* Toronto: Lorimer, 2007.

Paul, Jason. "Canadian Coach Gets Vindication— Miller Clear in James' Affair." *Toronto Sun,* December 19, 1997, sec. sports, p. 141.

Paul, Jason. "Veteran James Stunned by Her Exclusion." *Toronto Sun,* December 10, 1997, sec.sports, p. 18.

Russell, Scott. *Ice Time: A Canadian Hockey Journey.* Toronto: Viking, 2000.

The Black Ice Project:"The Black Hockey and Sports Hall of Fame" URL:http://www.theblackiceproject.com/blackiceproject/index. cfm?fuseaction=home.newsDetail&NEWS_ID=307 [03.01.11]

"Three Senecans inducted into OCAA Hall of Fame." *Seneca Alumni Magazine,* 2005. Vol. 2.

Warmington, Joe."Livid James Lashes Out," *Calgary Sun,* 11 December 1997, sec. sports, p. 115.

Wright, Lyn (1997). *The Game of Her Life.* National Film Board of Canada/CBC Sports,

Zwolinski, Mark. "James Presents Her Case." *The Toronto Star,* December 17, 1997. sec. sports, p. E9.

ACKNOWLEDGMENTS

The authors would like to thank all those who contributed to this book through interviews and consultation, including: Ray Bennett, Robin Brown, Jean Bryant, Judy Butler, Cassie Campbell-Pascall, Murray Costello, Melody Davidson, Ken Dufton, Elizabeth Etue, Cammi Granato, Adam Graves, Bill Humber, Laurie Ikeda, Leo James, Bob Nicholson, Cathy Phillips, Fran Rider, Linda Stapleton, Lee Trempe, Sarah Wayne and Hayley Wickenheiser. We would also like to note that Shannon Miller did not respond to our requests for an interview.

A special thank you to Angela, Ange, Donna, Cindy and Kym for their openness, candidness and willingness to share their inspiring stories.

Tom Bartsiokas is a writer, editor and communications specialist at Seneca College. Since 2005, he has been the editor of The Senecan, the College's campus news publication as well as a regular contributor to RED, Seneca's alumni magazine.

When he is not typing away on his computer, Tom also teaches part-time in the School of English and Liberal Studies at Seneca. He lives in Toronto with his wife, Christine, and their daughters Angelina, Deanna and Elena.

Corey Long is an administrator and part-time teacher at Seneca College, as well as a writer and editor for the alumni publication RED. He grew up in Alliston, Ontario, and has studied in the United States and Norway. Corey lives in Newmarket, Ontario with his wife, Shannon, and their daughter Clara.